Pick a Chord

Bert Weedon's

**SHORT CUT GUITAR GUIDE
WITH INSTANT CHORD FINDER**

A NEW GUITAR METHOD FOR INSTANT CHORD PLAYING
GIVING ALL BASIC CHORDS AND EXTENDED CHORDS.
IDEAL FOR BEGINNERS, INVALUABLE FOR EXPERIENCED PLAYERS.

AF079284

FABER *ff* MUSIC

© 2013 by Faber Music Ltd
First published by Chappell Music in 1979
Bloomsbury House
74–77 Great Russell Street
London WC1B 3DA
Printed in England by Caligraving Ltd
All rights reserved

ISBN10: 0-571-53834-7
EAN13: 978-0-571-53834-8

Reproducing this music in any form is illegal and forbidden by
the Copyright, Designs and Patents Act, 1988

This paper is 100% recyclable

To buy Faber Music publications or to find out about the full range of titles available
please contact your local retailer or Faber Music sales enquiries:

Faber Music Limited, Burnt Mill, Elizabeth Way, Harlow, CM20 2HX England
Tel: +44 (0) 1279 82 89 82   Fax: +44 (0) 1279 82 89 83
sales@fabermusic.com   fabermusicstore.com

PICK A CHORD

Introduction

In writing this new book I hope that I am fulfilling a need that has been in existence for a long time. There are many people who love the sound of a guitar, and who would like to be able to accompany themselves or others, but who do not have the time to make a full-time study of the instrument. The guitar is a lifetime study if one wishes to play solos of a high standard, but for those who would like to play simple accompaniments, a very pleasant sound can be obtained in surprisingly little time if one knows the short cuts. It is these that I hope to demonstrate to you in the following pages of this book.

Pick A Chord is not designed to teach you to play solos; for anyone wanting to play in this style I would refer them to my book **Play In A Day**; but it will teach you all the simple chords you will require for playing any kind of music — pop, country and western, folk, rock and roll, etc. This new **Short Cut** method will enable you to make music with your guitar quickly, and give pleasure to your listeners when you play. Because it is a short cut method, I am going to by-pass all the rudiments of musical theory, and go straight on to playing the simple chords that are used in every tune. Later in the book you will find a comprehensive list of many extended chords together with some simple alternatives. In this way **Pick A Chord** will be very useful for both the experienced player (who needs to know more about playing the more complicated chords that one sometimes comes across) and the beginner.

I hope that you will get a lot of pleasure from learning to play the guitar with the help of this book and I know you will be surprised at how quickly you are able to play. Don't delay until tomorrow turn over the page and START!

PICK A CHORD

PART 1

Page
- **3**   Introduction
- **6**   Guitars and Strings — How the Guitar is Tuned; Holding the Guitar; Strumming.
- **10**   Chords and Chord Symbols — Playing your first Chords; Accompanying your first song.
- **15**   More new Chords and songs, Minor Chords and barring; The 12 Bar Blues.
- **25**   First steps in bass note picking.

PART 2

- **28**   All the basic chords and fingering diagrams.

PART 3

- **46**   Extended chords for the advanced player; and some easy easy alternatives for the beginner.
- **64**   And in conclusion . . .

GUITARS AND STRINGS

As I said in the introduction, I am not going to deal with the rudiments of musical theory in detail. This is a **Short Cut** method and will go straight on to playing chords but before that, here are a few notes about guitars generally.

It does not matter what kind of guitar you have to learn on. All guitars are tuned the same, and they all have six strings (except the twelve-string guitar which is a separate instrument). There are two main types of guitar: One has steel strings, and the other has nylon strings — both types are tuned and fingered in the same way by the left hand.

Guitars with steel strings have a louder tone, and are mainly used for pop and country and western music, although they can of course be used to play any kind of music. Only guitars with steel strings can be played as electric guitars — steel strings can be used with an electric magnetic pick up, whereas, of course, nylon strings are not suitable for this purpose.

It does not matter whether your guitar has a round sound-hole in the middle of the body, or whether it has 'f'-holes cut into the body like a violin or cello — their purpose is merely to vary the tone of the guitar. A guitar with a round sound-hole has a richer and fuller sound while a guitar with 'f'-holes has a more penetrating and incisive sound — both types are good, and it is a matter of taste which you choose. As I have already said they are both fingered exactly the same with the left hand. It is with the right hand that the way of playing can be varied.

It is usual to play a steel-stringed guitar with a plectrum. A plectrum is a piece of tortoiseshell or plastic (see illustration 1) used to strike across the strings. It is held by the thumb and first finger of the right hand, with the tip of the plectrum protruding about a quarter of an inch (see illustration 2). It is, of course, quite possible to play a steel-stringed guitar with the fingers but a plectrum on the whole is preferable, and it improves the tone quality. Also strumming this type of guitar with the fingers will tend to make them sore.

Guitars with nylon strings are usually played with the fingers of the right hand rather than with a plectrum, as the nylon strings are much softer to the touch and this of course accounts for the difference in tone between the two types of guitars. The nylon-stringed instrument is soft and sweet in tone, and the guitar with steel strings is louder and more incisive.

How the Guitar is Tuned

The strings of the guitar are tuned to the notes E A D G B E starting with the thickest string. This string (E — on the far left in all the diagrams shown in this book) is known as the 6th string; and the next string, the 5th string is tuned to A; the 4th string to D; the 3rd string to G; and the 2nd string to B; finally the thinnest and 1st string is tuned to E. Of course the E to which the 6th string is tuned is two octaves deeper than the E to which the 1st string is tuned, but, to avoid going into musical theory and to get on quickly with playing, I suggest that in order to tune the guitar the reader buys some pitch pipes from any music shop. These are six little pipes joined together, tuned to the six strings of the guitar. Each pipe is blown separately and you tune the relative string to the note given by the pipe by raising or lowering the pitch of the string until it sounds the same as the note given by the pipe. To change the pitch of a string you turn the tuning key one way to lower the note, and the opposite way to raise the note. Pitch Pipes are not expensive and can be carried around with your guitar so as always to be available.

For those who prefer tuning to a piano I have indicated the method over .

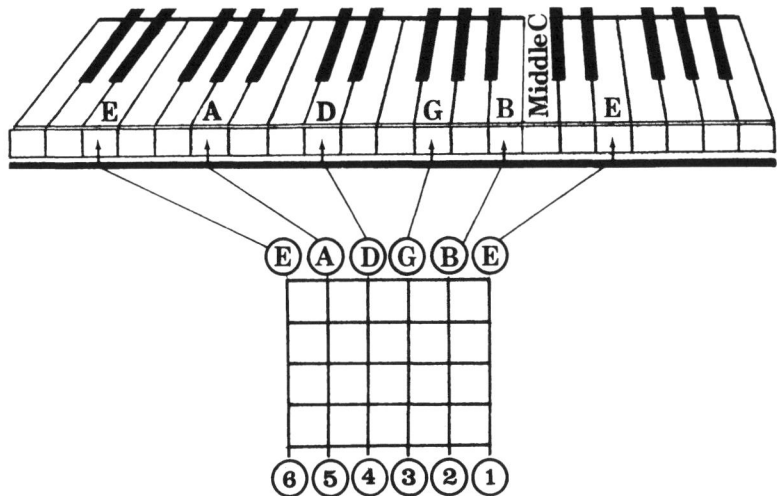

There are also various electronic tuning devices available in some musical equipment shops. They are very efficient, but rather expensive, and so for the beginner I suggest the use of pitch pipes.

Holding the Guitar

Having tuned the guitar it is now necessary to learn how to hold it correctly. The player may either sit or stand. If he is seated it is best to have the left knee raised by resting the left foot on a stool or some object about six inches high. The curve in the body of the guitar will then rest on the left leg just above the knee. The guitar is then in a suitable position for the left hand to finger the strings easily, and for the right hand to strum.

Most players, however, prefer to play standing up, and for this a shoulder strap is needed. These are available from most music shops and the photograph shows how it is worn.

Strumming

As learning to strum is the first step in this 'short cut' method of playing the guitar; musical theory can be set aside for the time being. When strumming on a nylon string guitar use the nail of the first finger, or the ball (or fleshy) part of the thumb. Whichever way you use, however, make the strokes even as you strike downwards and practise striking across the strings so that you can get a smooth easy movement with the right hand wrist. Do not let your wrist become stiff and taut — relax and strum across the strings easily and smoothly, striking them just hard enough to give a pleasant tone. Do not bother at this stage to do any fingering with your left hand, just practise the strumming action. If you are using a plectrum, hold it as in illustration 2, gripping just firmly enough so that it glides across the strings. Whichever way you have decided to play however always strike down across the strings with a regular beat, keeping a steady rhythm. To indicate a stroke (strum) across the strings we use the following sign: ✔ Two signs like this: ✔✔ would mean two strums and so on.

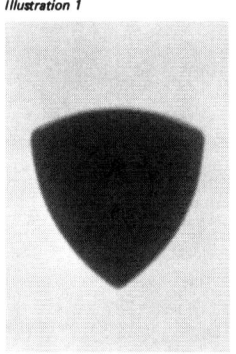
Illustration 1

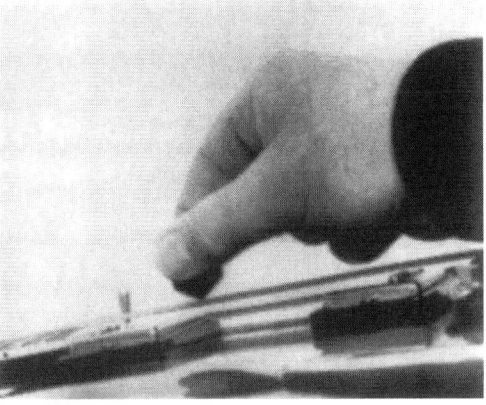
Illustration 2

Most popular music has either three or four beats to the bar, and it is the number of beats (or strums across the strings) that gives a tune its rhythm. A waltz rhythm such as 'Moon River' for instance has three beats to a bar, whereas a piece like 'Rock around the Clock' has four beats to a bar.

Try humming both tunes and tapping out the beat and you will see what I mean.

To indicate the number of beats to each bar, we put the stroke signs between two upright lines called bar lines. This | ✔ ✔ ✔ ✔ | indicates four strums or strokes to the bar and this | ✔ ✔ ✔ | indicates you would play three strokes. When you start practising strumming across the strings I suggest you begin with three beats to a bar. As you strike the strings count to yourself: One, two, three; one, two, three; one, two, three etc. Also try striking slightly harder every time you strum the first beat of each three; this will help you feel the rhythm:

    ONE, two, three,   ONE, two, three,   ONE, two three

Now try counting four beats to a bar and this time strike the first and third beats louder. Again this gives a rhythmic 'feel' to the music:

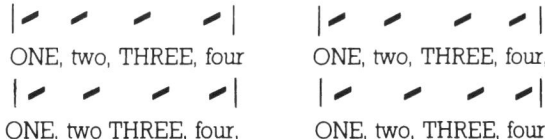

  ONE, two, THREE, four   ONE, two, THREE, four,

  ONE, two THREE, four,   ONE, two, THREE, four.

Remember to count regularly as you strike across the strings whether you are playing three or four beats to each bar. Don't worry that the strings produce a discordant sound as you strike them — this is because you are not as yet fingering a chord with your left hand. Remember this is only a strumming exercise for your right hand. We will deal with the actual fingering of the chords later.

Whilst I am on the subject of bar lines let me give you one or two more points. When a piece is finished it is usual to write a Double Bar Line thus ‖ and you will see examples of this in all the songs in this book. If you see a Double Bar Line with two dots after it thus ‖: , it means that the bars following this sign should be played until you get to a Double Bar Line with two dots before it :‖ , and then the whole section of music enclosed by these signs should be repeated. In the following example the first six bars would be repeated and then the final two bars would finish off the piece.

‖: ⟋ ⟋ ⟋ ⟋ | ⟋ ⟋ ⟋ ⟋ | ⟋ ⟋ ⟋ ⟋ | ⟋ ⟋ ⟋ ⟋ | ⟋ ⟋ ⟋ ⟋ | ⟋ ⟋ ⟋ ⟋ :‖ ⟋ ⟋ ⟋ ⟋ | ⟋ ⟋ ⟋ ⟋ ‖

CHORDS AND CHORD SYMBOLS

When three or more notes are played together in harmony they are called Chords, and it is by strumming various chords that we get the different harmonies to the tunes being played.

Until recent years there was only one way of writing down which chords should be played, and that was by using traditional musical notation. A quick and easy method of writing chords however has now been generally adopted, and the use of **Chord Symbols** is now common practice. These work in the following way.

Every chord has a letter to identify it. The letters used are the first seven letters of the alphabet — A B C D E F G — which are the names of the notes used in music. Each of these letters identifies a certain chord. Very often however a letter will be accompanied by a number or some other indication of a change to the chord. Take for example the letter C, (although of course any other letter from A to G could have been used). If the letter C is written alone, it means that the chord of C major is to be played. If the symbol is written Cm (or sometimes it is written as Cmin), then that indicates that the chord of C minor is to be played. If the symbol is written C7, then it means that the chord of C7 is to be played. I will show you how to play these chords later in the book.

There are only five main types of basic chords used in music: **major** chords (written C), **minor** chords (written Cm or Cmin), **seventh** chords (written C7), **diminished** chords (written Cdim or C°), and **augmented chords (written** Caug or C+). Again, in the examples just given the letter C has been used, but any letter from A to G could have been used; the same rules apply to any letter used. Various extensions or additions to these basic chords are often made by adding extra notes to form more sophisticated harmony; but it is quite all right for the beginner to play a basic chord instead of the more complicated one and this will be explained fully later in the book. Extended chords will also be dealt with later on; the fingerings for the five basic chord shapes will be found in Part 2.

And one more point: As already mentioned, all chords are based on and named after the first seven letters of the alphabet — A B C D E F G — but it is possible to raise the pitch or sound of these chords by adding a 'sharp' sign ♯. Therefore a chord symbol such as C♯ means you would play the chord of C sharp major. In other words adding a sharp sign after any chord symbol makes the chord into a 'sharp' chord and it will sound a little higher in pitch. It is also possible to add a flat sign, ♭, after a chord symbol as in for example E♭ (which means E flat major). So remember any chord can be raised in pitch by adding a sharp sign (♯) or lowered in pitch by adding a flat sign (♭), and this rule applies not only to major chords, but to all chords i.e. major, minor, seventh diminished and augmented.

Playing Your First Chords

The chord shapes given in this book are illustrated in the following way. The diagrams show the six strings of the guitar running vertically together. The lowest sounding string — the **thickest** string — is on the extreme left and the highest sounding string — the **thinnest** string — is on the right hand side of the diagram. This will enable you to identify the strings for the purpose of fingering. The strings are also numbered like this:

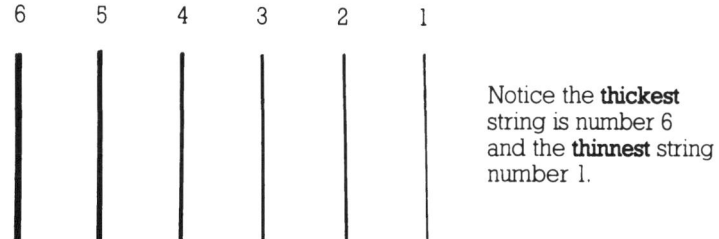

Notice the **thickest** string is number 6 and the **thinnest** string number 1.

Across the six strings shown in the diagrams are drawn some horizontal lines. These represent the frets on the fingerboard of the guitar. Frets are pieces of wire that are set at intervals across the fingerboard and their purpose is to create different pitches of notes when the strings are pressed down or (to use the correct term) 'stopped' behind the frets. Please note that the string is always 'stopped' **behind** and not on top of the fret.

The top horizontal line on the diagrams is not a fret but represents the nut — the part of the guitar over which the strings pass at the tuning keys end of the fingerboard. This is usually made of wood or bone (sometimes plastic). In the diagram it can easily be identified as it is **much** thicker than the frets.

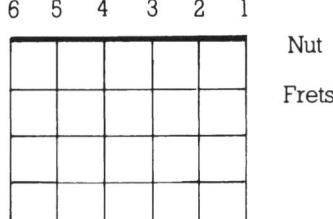

Finally, having explained the diagrams showing the strings and frets, round dots are now inserted which indicate where to put the tips of the fingers of the left hand. The fingers are numbered as follows: the first (or index) finger is number 1, the middle finger is number 2, the third finger number 3, and the small finger number 4. And of course the correct finger must **always** be used. The sign O above a string means that the string is not fingered at all, and that it should be played 'open' or unfingered. And now for your first chord!

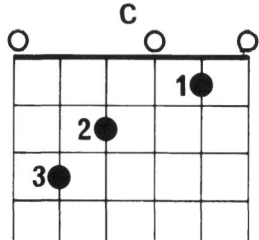

Having checked that the guitar is in tune have a look at the chord shape shown (which is the chord of C). Remember, when you press the strings down with the tips of the fingers, press just behind the fret, and not immediately on top of it. A little experimenting and listening to the sound you make will show whether you are doing this correctly. (If you press the strings down just behind the fret the note will be clear and ringing, whereas if the strings are pressed down on the top of the fret the note is not as clear). Always use a reasonable amount of pressure when pressing the strings down; if the string is not pressed down firmly it will not produce a clear sound but will 'buzz'. Remember that everyone has some trouble at first in 'stopping' a string but with a little practice (and believe me it will not take long) you will be able to play chords quite easily.

Once you have remembered where to put your fingers on the strings, practice taking them off and putting them on again so as to become thoroughly familiar with the chord shape, and it will be surprising how quickly you will be able to play the chords correctly. When pressing down the strings use only the tips of the left-hand fingers, and make sure that your finger does not accidentally come into contact with the next string, otherwise it will stop it from sounding. A little practice in placing the tips of the fingers on the strings will ensure you do it correctly.

Having fingered the chord it is now time to play it. Reread what has been said about strumming and playing in time and then take a plectrum, or use the nail of your first finger, or the tip of the thumb of your right hand and try a few strokes of the chord C as shown. Try and memorise the position of the left hand fingers so that whenever you see the chord symbol C you will be able to play it without hesitation. Make sure your fingers are pressed down firmly and strum rhythmically with the right hand. Remember music is always divided into bars in order to give a particular beat, and most popular music has either three or four beats to every bar. If three beats are written to every bar as shown here, then the first of every three beats should be played a little louder than the following two beats in order to give a lilt to the rhythm:

```
   C         C         C         C
|✓ ✓ ✓ |✓ ✓ ✓ |✓ ✓ ✓ |✓ ✓ ✓ |
```

If four beats are written to the bar, then the first and third beats should be louder. (As an alternative one can sometimes reverse the order and accent the second and fourth beats to give a different beat to the rhythm. Try it and see.)

```
   C           C           C           C
|✓ ✓ ✓ ✓ |✓ ✓ ✓ ✓ |✓ ✓ ✓ ✓ |✓ ✓ ✓ ✓ |
```

Occasionally you will find a chord symbol written in place of one of the strokes and this must be counted as a beat. This method is often adopted to save time and space. Thus the following would be played as four beats of the chord of C because we are counting the symbol as one beat.

```
|C ✓ ✓ ✓ |C ✓ ✓ ✓ |C ✓ ✓ ✓ |C ✓ ✓ ✓ |
```

It would sound the same if it were written:

```
   C            C            C            C
|✓ ✓ ✓ ✓ |✓ ✓ ✓ ✓ |✓ ✓ ✓ ✓ |✓ ✓ ✓ ✓ |
```

This example would be played as three strokes of the chord.

```
|C ✓ ✓ |C ✓ ✓ |C ✓ ✓ |C ✓ ✓ |
```

It would sound the same if it were written:

```
   C         C         C         C
|✓ ✓ ✓ |✓ ✓ ✓ |✓ ✓ ✓ |✓ ✓ ✓ |
```

Now let us try another chord shape — here is the fingering for G7.

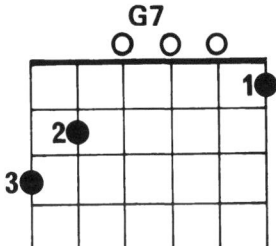

Notice the same fingers are used as for C — but they are in different positions. Try remembering the position of the fingers for G7, and practice fingering this chord and learning where to put the fingers of the left hand so that when you see the chord symbol G7 you will play the correct chord shape automatically. After you have mastered the fingering try playing the chord to a steady beat as you did with C. Then try the following exercise: Start off with two bars of C, then two bars of G7, then two of C, etc. Try and make the change from one chord to another without losing the beat. You will find you have to pause at first, but after some practice you will be able to move from one chord to another easily.

```
|C ✓ ✓ |C ✓ ✓ ✓ |G7 ✓ ✓ ✓ |G7 ✓ ✓ ✓ |C ✓ ✓ ✓ |C ✓ ✓ ✓ |G7 ✓ ✓ ✓ |G7 ✓ ✓ ✓|
```

Now let us try changing the chord every bar.

```
|C ✓ ✓ ✓ |G7 ✓ ✓ ✓ |C ✓ ✓ ✓ |G7 ✓ ✓ ✓ |C ✓ ✓ ✓ |G7 ✓ ✓ ✓ |C ✓ ✓ ✓ |G7 ✓ ✓ ✓||
```

Now try changing the chord every two beats.

```
|C ✓ G7 ✓ |C ✓ G7 ✓ |C ✓ G7 ✓ |C ✓ G7 ✓ |C ✓ G7 ✓ |C ✓ G7 ✓ |C ✓ G7 ✓ |C ✓ G7 ✓||
```

Accompanying Your First Song

It is likely that every reader will know the melody of Bobby Shaftoe, and here are the chords together with the words so that you can try singing the melody as you strum the accompaniment. Try making the change from one chord to another smoothly without holding up the beat or rhythm of the piece. You will have to practice! — but you will find that you will be able to do it quite easily after a while. Try thinking ahead all the time, and prepare your mind for the next chord change **before you actually get to it**, and you will find that before very long your fingers will go quickly to the right strings and positions. Before you start, make sure you have memorised the fingering for both chord symbols and notice that the song has four beats to every bar. Then, strum the chord of C a few times and, keeping the same finger position, pluck the first string. This will give you your first note for 'Bob' (of 'Bobby') and that is the note on which you start singing and strumming.

Bobby Shaftoe

```
Bob - by   Shaf - toe's    gone  to   sea . . . . . ,
|C     ⌐      ⌐      ⌐    |C    ⌐    ⌐    ⌐    |

Sil - ver  buck - les     on   his   knee . . . . ,
|G7    ⌐     ⌐     ⌐      |G7   ⌐    ⌐    ⌐    |

He'll come back  and      mar - ry   me . . . . ,
|C      ⌐    ⌐    ⌐       |C    ⌐    ⌐    ⌐    |

Bon - nie  Bob - by        Shaf - toe . . . . . .
|G7    ⌐     ⌐     ⌐      |C    ⌐    ⌐    ⌐    |
```

Now for a tune with three beats to the bar: 'Down in the Valley' which as most of you will realise is in Waltz time. Remember to play the first beat of every bar a little louder than the following two beats in order to give the tune a pleasant lilt. Also you need to sing the words 'Down in the' before you begin to strum the accompaniment. So, as in the previous song, strum the chord of C a few times and (always keeping the same finger position!) pluck the 3rd string. This will give you the note for 'Down'.

Down in the Valley

```
Down in the val  - ley . . . . . . . . . . . . val-ley so low . . . . . . . . . . . . . . . . . Hang your head
            |C  ⌐ ⌐ |C  ⌐ ⌐ |C  ⌐ ⌐ |C  ⌐ ⌐  |G7 ⌐ ⌐ |G7 ⌐ ⌐ |G7 ⌐ ⌐ |G7  ⌐  ⌐|

        O  -  ver . . . . . . . . . . . hear the wind blow . . . . . . . . . . . . . . . . Hear the wind
|G7 ⌐ ⌐ |G7 ⌐ ⌐ |G7 ⌐ ⌐ |G7 ⌐  ⌐ |C ⌐ ⌐  |C ⌐ ⌐  |C ⌐ ⌐  |C  ⌐  ⌐ |

blow . . . love . . . . . . . . . . . Hear the wind blow . . . . . . . . . . . . . . . . . Hang your head
|C ⌐ ⌐ |C  ⌐ ⌐ |C ⌐ ⌐ |C ⌐   ⌐ |G7 ⌐ ⌐ |G7 ⌐ ⌐ |G7 ⌐ ⌐ |G7  ⌐  ⌐|

        o  -  ver . . . . . . . . . . , Hear the wind blow . . . . . . . . . . . . . . . . . . . . . . . . .
|G7 ⌐ ⌐ |G7 ⌐ ⌐ |G7 ⌐ ⌐ |G7 ⌐  ⌐ |C ⌐ ⌐  |C ⌐ ⌐  |C ⌐ ⌐  |C ⌐ ⌐ ||
```

MORE NEW CHORDS AND SONGS

It is necessary to learn two more chord shapes: G (i.e. G major) and D7 for the next song. Notice that in the diagram for D7 the lowest or thickest string has an X over it. This is to indicate that the lowest string should **not** be played or struck with the other strings — in other words you must only play the top five strings for this chord. This is a rule that applies throughout the book: if you see an 'X' over any string it means that this string should **not** be played.

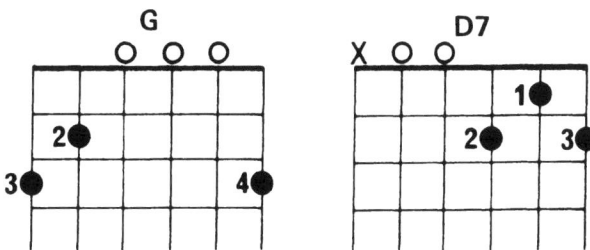

Again the student should memorise the finger positions and aim to make the change from one chord to the other smoothly and easily. When you have mastered the change try the following tune, which has four beats to each bar. For this tune, strum the chord of G a few times, and take your first note from the 2nd string.

Polly Wolly Doodle

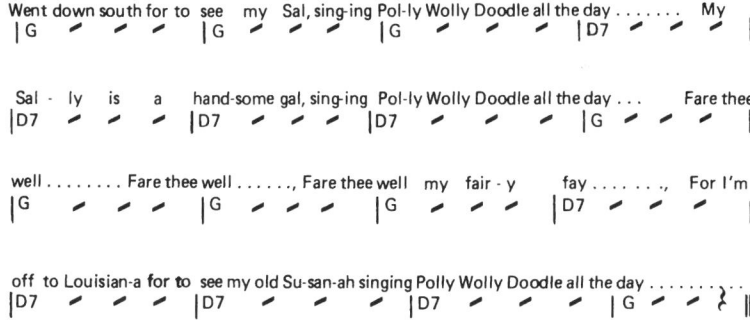

Notice the rest sign ⸘ in the last bar. This means do not play on this beat but count the beat as a silent one, so only play three strums on the last bar: the last beat is silent.

You will often see a rest sign in the following pages and each time you see this sign it means the beat should be counted but not played. Here is a song incorporating three chords. Before you begin, strum the chord of G a few times, and pluck the 4th string. This is your note for the word 'Camptown'.

Camptown Races

```
Camp-town lad-ies     sing this song....   Doo-dah........   Doo-dah..... the
| G  ♩  ♩  ♩      | G  ♩  ♩  ♩      | D7  ♩  ♩  ♩     | D7  ♩  ♩  ♩     |

Camp-town race track's five miles long....   Oh.....Doo dah day..........  I
| G  ♩  ♩  ♩      | G  ♩  ♩  ♩      | D7  ♩  ♩  ♩     | G  ♩  ♩  ♩      |

came down with my    hat caved in.....   Doo-dah........   Doo-dah..... I
| G  ♩  ♩  ♩      | G  ♩  ♩  ♩      | D7  ♩  ♩  ♩     | D7  ♩  ♩  ♩     |

go back home with a pocket full of tin....  Oh.....Doo-dah day............
| G  ♩  ♩  ♩      | G  ♩  ♩  ♩      | D7  ♩  ♩  ♩     | G  ♩  ♩  ♩      |

CHORUS
Goin' to run all     night..........,     Goin to run all  day........,  I
| G  ♩  ♩  ♩      | G  ♩  ♩  ♩      | C  ♩  ♩  ♩      | G  ♩  ♩  ♩      |

bet my money on the Bob Tail nag....,  Some-bo-dy bet on the Bay........
| G  ♩  ♩  ♩      | G  ♩  ♩  ♩      | D7  ♩  ♩  ♩     | G  ♩  ♩  𝄽     |
```

Note again we have a rest sign in the last bar, so only three strums in this bar. Here is a song which uses four chords: play the chord of G and the 4th string will give you your first note.

There is a Tavern in the Town

```
There's......a     tav-ern in the  town... in the  town......., and
| G  ♩  ♩  ♩    | G  ♩  ♩  ♩    | G  ♩  ♩  ♩    | G  ♩  ♩  ♩       |

There......my    dear love sits him  down....sits him down.... And he
| G  ♩  ♩  ♩    | G  ♩  ♩  ♩    | D7  ♩  ♩  ♩   | D7  ♩  ♩  ♩      |

drinks...his.....  wine....mid.....  laugh-ter..... free........ and
| G  ♩  ♩  ♩    | G7  ♩  ♩  ♩   | C  ♩  ♩  ♩    | C  ♩  ♩  ♩       |

Nev-er           nev-er thinks of   me...................... Fare thee
| D7  ♩  ♩  ♩   | D7  ♩  ♩  ♩   | G  ♩  ♩  ♩    | G  ♩  ♩  ♩       |

well for I must  leave thee do not   let the part-ing grieve thee and re-
| D7  ♩  ♩  ♩   | D7  ♩  ♩  ♩   | G  ♩  ♩  ♩    | G  ♩  ♩  ♩       |

mem-ber that the  best of friends must part.....must..... part........, A-
| D7  ♩  ♩  ♩   | D7  ♩  ♩  ♩   | G  ♩  C  ♩    | G  ♩  ♩  ♩       |

dieu.........A-  dieu kind friends A-dieu,  A-dieu, A-dieu........  I
| G  ♩  ♩  ♩    | G  ♩  ♩  ♩    | G  ♩  ♩  ♩    | G  ♩  ♩  ♩       |

can..........no  long-er stay with  you.....stay with you.... and I'll
| G  ♩  ♩  ♩    | G  ♩  ♩  ♩    | D7  ♩  ♩  ♩   | D7  ♩  ♩  ♩      |

hang......my.....harp..... on   a   weep-ing will-ow tree........, and
| G  ♩  ♩  ♩    | G7  ♩  ♩  ♩   | C  ♩  ♩  ♩    | C  ♩  ♩  ♩       |

may........the  world go well with thee.............................
| D7  ♩  ♩  ♩   | D7  ♩  ♩  ♩   | G  ♩  ♩  ♩    | G  ♩  ♩  𝄽    ||
```

Here are two more chord shapes to learn. They are the chords of D and A7, and they are fingered as shown.

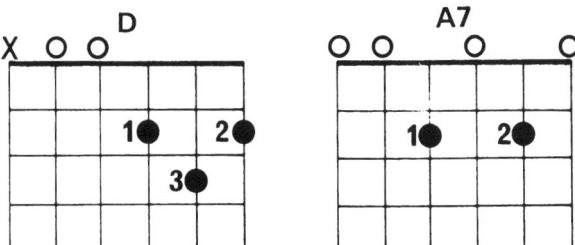

These chord shapes are incorporated straight away into a new tune — the traditional song 'Frankie and Johnny': again it's four beats to the bar, and the 4th string when you play the chord of D will give you your first note.

Frankie and Johnny

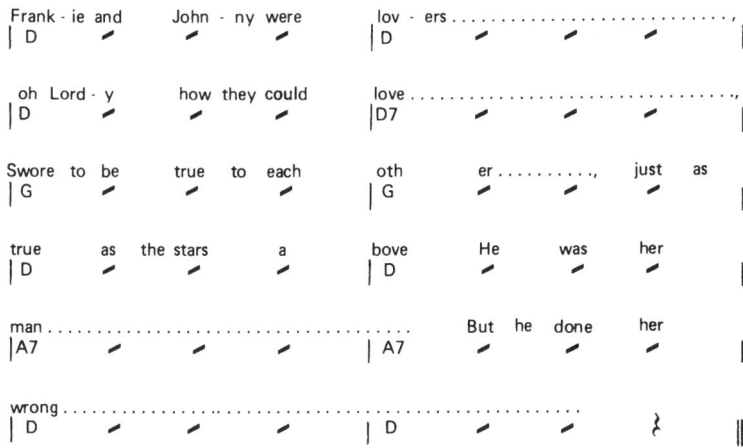

Your next two chord shapes are A and E7. Again memorise the fingering and try the following well-known tune. The 2nd string when you play the chord of A will give you the note for 'She'll'. Note that you do not start strumming until you have sung 'She'll be'.

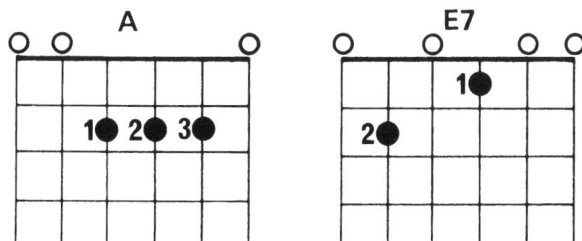

She'll Be Coming Round The Mountain

She'll be coming round the moun-tain when she comes........., ...She'll be
|A ⁄ ⁄ ⁄ |A ⁄ ⁄ ⁄ |A ⁄ ⁄ ⁄ |A ⁄ ⁄ ⁄ |

com - ing round the moun-tain when she   comes............, ...She'll be
|A ⁄ ⁄ ⁄ |A ⁄ ⁄ ⁄ |E7 ⁄ ⁄ ⁄ |E7 ⁄ ⁄ ⁄ |

com - ing round the   moun-tain........, com - ing round the   moun - tain........,
|A ⁄ ⁄ ⁄ |A7 ⁄ ⁄ ⁄ |D ⁄ ⁄ ⁄ |D ⁄ ⁄ ⁄ |

com - ing round the   moun - tain when she   comes...........................
|A ⁄ ⁄ ⁄ |E7 ⁄ ⁄ ⁄ |A ⁄ ⁄ ⁄ |A ⁄ ⁄ ⁀ ||

'When the Saints Come Marching In' uses the chords A, E7, A7 and D. The tune has four beats to the bar. For this tune the 3rd string when you play the chord of A, will give you the note for "Oh".

When the Saints Come Marching In

Oh when the Saints......... ...come marching in..........., ... Oh when the
|A ⁄ ⁄ ⁄ |A ⁄ ⁄ ⁄ |A ⁄ ⁄ ⁄ |A ⁄ ⁄ ⁄ |

Saints... come.... march - ing..... in..............., ...I'm going to
|A ⁄ ⁄ ⁄ |A ⁄ ⁄ ⁄ |E7 ⁄ ⁄ ⁄ |E7 ⁄ ⁄ ⁄ |

be.... there..... in.... their..... num-ber........., ...When the
|A ⁄ ⁄ ⁄ |A7 ⁄ ⁄ ⁄ |D ⁄ ⁄ ⁄ |D ⁄ ⁄ ⁄ |

Saints... come..... march − ing..... in................ ....
|A ⁄ ⁄ ⁄ |E7 ⁄ ⁄ ⁄ |A ⁄ ⁄ ⁄ |A ⁄ ⁄ ⁀ ||

Now try a tune with a stronger rhythm using the chords D, A7, D7 and G. It's an old tune that's been played in just about every possible way. Play it with a strong four-to-a-bar beat. The notes for 'Gonna' can be taken from the 2nd string when you play the chord of D, and the note for 'lay' is that given by the 1st string.

Down by the Riverside

So far the following chords C, G7, G, D7, D, A7, A and E7 have been learnt, and the reader will have noticed that with them it is possible to accompany several tunes (in fact with just these few chords there are hundreds of songs that can be played quite easily).

Minor Chords

As mentioned before these are indicated by 'm' or 'min' after the letter name of the chord; 'm' or 'min' of course are simply shortened versions of 'minor'. For the purposes of this book I will only use 'm' — but you must learn to recognise both alternatives!

Most people think a minor chord has a rather sad sound about it as opposed to a major chord, which sounds somewhat brighter. Try playing A (major) and then Am and see if you can hear the difference. The major chord is bright and the minor chord is rather sad and wistful. Here are your first two minor chords — Am and Em:

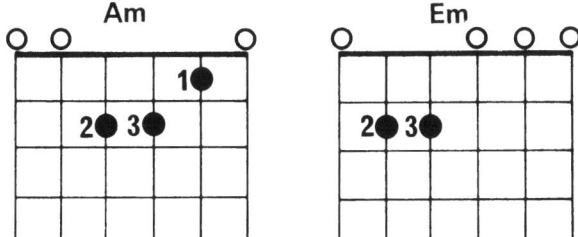

Press each finger down firmly to ensure a nice clean sound — and remember not to touch (accidentally) the open strings or they will not 'sing'. The following tune incorporates these two new chords.

It is the old folk song called 'The Riddle Song'. The same chords can also be played for the pop version of the song called 'The Twelfth of Never'. The 4th string when you play the chord of G will give you the note for 'I', which is also the note for 'gave' when you start to strum.

The Riddle Song

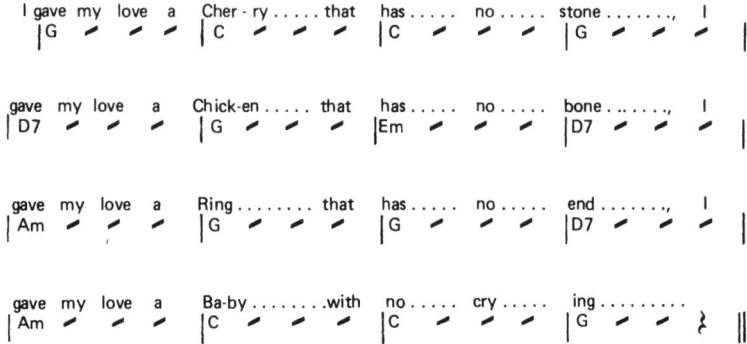

```
I gave my love a    Cher-ry..... that    has..... no..... stone......,   I
|G   ✓  ✓  ✓         |C   ✓  ✓  ✓         |C   ✓  ✓  ✓      |G   ✓  ✓  ✓    |

gave my love a      Chick-en..... that   has..... no..... bone......,   I
|D7  ✓  ✓  ✓         |G   ✓  ✓  ✓         |Em  ✓  ✓  ✓      |D7  ✓  ✓  ✓    |

gave my love a      Ring........ that    has..... no..... end......,   I
|Am  ✓  ✓  ✓         |G   ✓  ✓  ✓         |G   ✓  ✓  ✓      |D7  ✓  ✓  ✓    |

gave my love a      Ba-by....... with    no..... cry..... ing........
|Am  ✓  ✓  ✓         |C   ✓  ✓  ✓         |C   ✓  ✓  ✓      |G   ✓  ✓  ⁀   ||
```

Here is another lovely folk song that has become a pop hit, it is called 'Scarboro' Fair'. Play it to a waltz rhythm with a slow, gentle three beats to every bar. The 4th string when you finger the chord of Em will give you the note for 'Are'.

Scarboro' Fair

```
Are...... you       go - ing   to       Scar - bor - o'    Fair.........,
|Em  ✓  ✓           |Em  ✓  ✓            |D   ✓  ✓          |Em  ✓  ✓        |

............ Pars - ley         Sage..... Rose - mar - y     and
|Em  ✓  ✓           |G   ✓  ✓            |Em  ✓  ✓          |A   ✓  ✓        |

Thyme........,      ......... Re - mem - - ber    me...... to
|Em  ✓  ✓           |Em  ✓  ✓            |Em  ✓  ✓          |G   ✓  ✓        |

one who lives       there.........,     ......... For    once...... She
|G   ✓  ✓           |D   ✓  ✓            |D   ✓  ✓          |Em  ✓  ✓        |

was...... a         true love of        mine.........      .............
|D   ✓  ✓           |D   ✓  ✓            |Em  ✓  ✓          |Em  ✓  ⁀        |
```

B7 is the next chord to learn. All four fingers of the left hand are used and you may find it a little difficult at first but with practice it will soon become easier to play. Here is the chord shape.

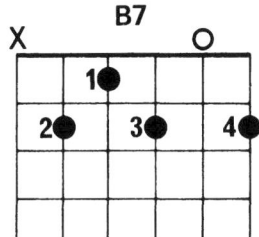

... and a piece that gives you an opportunity to practice the B7 shape. Again the tune is a folk song that has become a pop standard. This time the song has four beats to a bar. For this tune, strum the chord of Em a few times. In this case the first two notes of the words 'There is' are given; keep the fingering of Em and sing 'There' to the note of the 2nd string, and 'is' to the note of the 1st string.

The House of the Rising Sun

Here is a tune that is probably the best known of all English folk songs, 'Greensleeves', and it gives you another chance to try the chord of B7 together with some of the chords already learnt. It is in three time and should be played softly and liltingly. To find your first note, strum the chord of B7 a few times, and take the note for 'A' (of 'Alas') from the 1st string when you finger the chord of B7; **But** remember, although you need this chord for your first note, the first chord that you play in Greensleeves is in fact the chord of Em.

Greensleeves

```
A - las   my love .. you  do ... me wrong .. to  cast ... me  off so dis-court-eous - ly .., And
| Em  ~ ~ | Em  ~ ~ | D  ~ ~ | D  ~ ~ | Em  ~ ~ | Em  ~ ~ | B7  ~ ~ | B7  ~ ~ |

 I .. have lov - ed you oh. ..  so  long .. de - light -  ing   in .. your comp - an - y . . . . . .
| Em  ~ ~ | Em  ~ ~ | D  ~ ~ | D  ~ ~ | Em  ~ ~ | B7  ~ ~ | Em  ~ ~ | Em  ~ ~ |

Green  -  sleeves    was all . . . .my  joy . . . .   Green . . .  sleeves . . was my . . . de - light . . . .
|  G  ~ ~ | G  ~ ~ | D  ~ ~ | D  ~ ~ | Em  ~ ~ | Em  ~ ~ | B7  ~ ~ | B7  ~ ~ |

Green  -  sleeves was my heart . . of  gold . . and who but my  La  -  dy   Green  -  sleeves.
|  G  ~ ~ | G   ~ ~ | D  ~ ~ | D  ~ ~ | Em  ~ ~ | B7  ~ ~ | Em  ~ ~ | Em ~ ≀ ||
```

A different kind of chord, you will often come across, is the chord of F. In the diagram you will see that for this chord the first finger of the left hand must press down on two strings. Obviously the tip of one finger cannot press down on two strings at the same time, so the chord shape is played by pressing the first finger flat across both strings. As this is a difficult chord shape, start by just pressing the two strings only with the flattened first finger in order to get the feel of it. It will seem strange at first but persevere and you will find that you will be able to press the two strings down quite easily after a while; then put the second and third fingers down in the positions marked on the diagram, and you will have the chord of F.

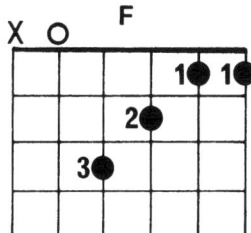

Having mastered the chord of F, now go on to the chord of Dminor which is somewhat easier to finger:

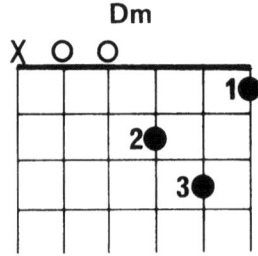

A musical sign that you will often come across and must be learned is the BAR REPEAT sign, which looks like this: | ✕ | It simply means that you repeat whatever has been written in the previous bar. Thus |c ✓ ✓ ✓ |c ✓ ✓ ✓ |c ✓ ✓ ✓ | could be written like this: |c ✓ ✓ ✓ | ✕ | ✕ | Learn the sign now!

12 Bar Blues

Now for a sequence of chords known as the 12 Bar Blues. A great many popular rock and roll songs are all based on the sequence of chords known as the 12 Bar Blues. Tunes like 'Rock around the Clock', 'Blue Suede Shoes', 'Be Bop a Lula', 'Johnny B. Goode', 'Shake Rattle and Roll', and instrumental hits like 'In the Mood', and 'Guitar Boogie Shuffle', are all based on this same sequence. The 12 Bar Blues may be played in any key, depending on the song you are singing and the pitch of your voice. Below are given the chords in three different keys. Try humming any of the tunes mentioned, and you'll find they are all based on the good old 12 Bar Blues. The bar repeat sign is used in these exercises to get you used to reading it. Remember it means repeat the previous bar, and if you see the sign again in the next bar, it merely means that once again you repeat the previous bar.

12 Bar Blues

Example 1

|G ✓ ✓ ✓ | ✕ | ✕ |G7 ✓ ✓ ✓ |C ✓ ✓ ✓ | ✕ |

|G ✓ ✓ ✓ | ✕ |D7 ✓ ✓ ✓ | ✕ |G ✓ ✓ ✓ | ✕ ||

Example 2

|D ✓ ✓ ✓ | ✕ | ✕ |D7 ✓ ✓ ✓ |G ✓ ✓ ✓ | ✕ |

|D ✓ ✓ ✓ | ✕ |A7 ✓ ✓ ✓ | ✕ |D ✓ ✓ ✓ | ✕ ||

Example 3

|A ✓ ✓ ✓ | ✕ | ✕ |A7 ✓ ✓ ✓ |D ✓ ✓ ✓ | ✕ |

|A ✓ ✓ ✓ | ✕ |E7 ✓ ✓ ✓ | ✕ |A ✓ ✓ ✓ | ✕ ||

Here is a piece of music that I am sure you will know called 'Michael Row the Boat Ashore', and it uses the two new chords just learnt. For this tune strum the chord of C a few times. The 5th and 4th strings when you play the chord of C will give you the first two notes of the tune (on the word 'Mich-ael').

Michael Row the Boat Ashore

Here is another tune which needs the chord of F. It is the old folk song 'On Top of Old Smokey'. Play the chord of C and take your starting note from the 5th string for the word 'On'. Note there are three beats to each bar and remember to strum a few chords of C to help you 'feel' the key.

On Top of Old Smokey

Notice the last bar has two rest signs so only play the first beat.

FIRST STEPS IN BASS NOTE PICKING

So far in all the tunes played you have strummed across the strings (with the exception of any strings marked with an 'X' above them). Another playing technique can now be learnt. This uses the right hand to pick a bass note (i.e. one of the lower strings of the chord) on the first beat, and then strum the top strings of the chord for the second and third beats.

This gives a nice waltz rhythm with the 1st beat on a bass note, and the 2nd and 3rd beats of the top strings. Use any of the lower strings of any chords that you are playing, but remember do not use a string with an 'X' above it — this will not sound in tune. You can use either the 6th, 5th or 4th string of any chord, providing it does not have an 'X' over it.

Let your ear be your guide as to which bass string you prefer, but as long as it is in the chord then it will sound pleasant. If you are playing with a plectrum, then pick the bass note separately, and then strum the rest of the chord with the next two strokes. If you are playing with your fingers, then pick the bass note downwards with your thumb and then either strike the remaining strings with the nail of the first finger, or pluck the top three strings with your first, second and third fingers. If you choose this method remember that your first finger plays the 3rd string, your second finger the 2nd string, and your third finger the 1st string, and with these three fingers pluck the strings upwards towards you; you pick the bass note downwards with your thumb tip. Here is the lovely old carol 'Silent Night'. To find the first note of the tune, play the chord of A and pluck the 4th string, this is the note you start on.

Silent Night

```
Si   -   lent      night . . . . . . . . . . ,     Ho  -  ly      night . . . . . . . . . . . . ,
| A      ↗    ↗    | A    ↗    ↗          | A    ↗    ↗     | A    ↗    ↗     |

All . . . . . . . is      calm . . . . . . . . . . . . ,     All . . . . . . . is      bright . . . . . . . . . . . . ,
| E7     ↗    ↗    | E7   ↗    ↗          | A    ↗    ↗     | A    ↗    ↗     |

Round        yon    vir   -   gin          Moth - er    and   child . . . . . . . . . . . . . ,
| D      ↗    ↗    | D    ↗    ↗          | A    ↗    ↗     | A    ↗    ↗     |

Ho.  -   ly       in  - fant   so          ten - der   and   mild . . . . . . . . . . . . ,
| D      ↗    ↗    | D    ↗    ↗          | A    ↗    ↗     | A    ↗    ↗     |

Sleep . . . . . . in    heav  - en  - ly   peace . . . . . . . . . . . . . . . . . . . . . . . . ,
| E7     ↗    ↗    | E7   ↗    ↗          | A    ↗    ↗     | A    ↗    ↗     |

Sleep . . . . . . in    heav  - en  - ly   peace . . . . . . . . . . . . . . . . . . . . . . . . . .
| A      ↗    ↗    | E7   ↗    ↗          | A    ↗    ↗     | A    ↗    ⸜     ||
```

Now try a tune with four beats to a bar, using the picked bass note style of playing. When playing in four time pick the bass note on the 1st and 3rd beats, and the top notes of the chord on the 2nd and 4th beats of the bar. Again let your ear be your guide, and remember to play only bass strings that are either fingered or are open strings (with an 'o' above them) — **Do not** play a bass string marked with an 'X'. Also try playing different notes on the 1st and 3rd beats. This always sounds good. For instance when playing the chord of A, pluck the 5th string on the 1st beat and the 6th string on the 3rd beat, and on the chord of E7 you could play again the 5th string on the 1st beat and the 6th string on the 3rd beat. (You will of course sometimes find that you are not fingering the 6th string in some chords, or that the 6th string has an 'X' over it, in which case you could alternate between the 4th and 5th strings for your bass notes.) Here is a piece using the chords of A and E7 and you can try varying the bass notes as suggested. The tune is 'He's got the whole World in His Hands'. The first string of the chord of A will give you your starting note and this note fits the first four words of the song, but do not start playing until the word 'whole'. Instead of strumming the first A chord, play the 5th string bass note on the first beat, then the full chord on the 2nd beat, then the 6th string bass note on the 3rd beat and the chord on the 4th beat and so on.

He's got the whole World in His Hands

He's got the	whole . . . . world	in his	hands, He's got the
	| A ∕ ∕ ∕	| A ∕	∕ ∕ |

whole . . . . world	in his	hands, He's got the
| E7 ∕ ∕ ∕	| E7 ∕	∕ ∕ |

whole . . . . world	in his	hands, He's got the
| A ∕ ∕ ∕	| A ∕	∕ ∕ |

whole world in his	hands	
| E7 ∕ ∕ ∕	| A ∕ ∕ 𝄾	||

Now that you have got the idea of playing in this style, try it out with some of the earlier tunes you have learnt.

As the space in this book is limited, I feel the reader will benefit more from the pages left at my disposal if I do not give any more examples of tunes with chords, as I feel by now you will have grasped both the idea and method of playing chords in time with the tunes and words. Therefore in the following pages I am going to deal with 'basic chord shapes'. Knowing these shapes will enable you to play simple accompaniments to more or less any tune.

Remember that the basic (or simple) chords are: **Major** written, for example, C; **Minor** written Cmin or Cm; **Seventh** written C7; **Diminished** written Cdim or C°and **Augmented** written Caug or C+. All printed popular music these days includes chord symbols. These indicate which chord to play as an accompaniment to the tune. The beginner must check each chord with its fingering and memorise it in order to be able to play the accompaniment fluently. All the basic chord shapes are shown in Part 2.

You will often find, however, different chords written on sheet music other than the five main basic chord shapes. They are known as extended chords, but they are all based on the basic chords, with extra notes added to them in order to give a more sophisticated sound. But beginners must not be deterred as most basic chord harmonies will still sound adequate when played as an alternative. In order that the beginner may know which basic chord to play as an alternative to the extended chords, a comprehensive list of many extended chords and opposite these the alternative basic chord which can be substituted for them, is given in Part 3. Of course, once the student has mastered and memorised all the basic chord shapes, he can then go on to learn and memorise the extended chord shapes, thereby enabling him to play the more sophisticated harmonies when he is ready to do so.

One type of extended chord, however, cannot be tastefully substituted with a basic chord, and it is a chord with a flattened 5th. There are two variations of this chord in general use, one is a seventh chord with a flattened 5th, written for example C7b5 or C7$^-$5, and the other variation is a minor seventh chord with a flattened 5th, written Cm7b5 or Cm7$^-$5. Both these shapes are shown in Part 3 in specially boxed-in diagrams opposite their basic chord and for these a basic chord **cannot** be played as an alternative to the given extended chord. For all the other extended chords I suggest that the beginner uses the basic chord alternative. The sound will always be quite adequate and of course the beginner will find this much easier.

Part 2

All the basic chords and fingering diagrams

In this section are diagrams for the five basic chords which can be formed on each letter name. In some of the diagrams it will be seen that one particular finger may have to hold down several strings at the same time (for example see the fingering for Fm or A7). This has occurred before, in the chord diagram for F. Reread that section before attempting any of these chords.

Remember all beginners **do** find this slightly difficult, but with practice it becomes quite easy once you have got the knack of pressing a finger down flat across several strings, whilst the other fingers press the strings down in the normal way, i.e. with the tips of the fingers. A chord that is played with a finger playing more than one string is called a **Barre** fingered chord. In the case of the chord A7, for instance, the diagram shows that the first finger presses down the 2nd, 3rd and 4th string together, but it should be noted that it is easier to press the top four strings down, i.e. the 1st, 2nd, 3rd and 4th with the first finger, and then to put the tip of the third finger on the 1st string where marked. It will not matter that the first finger as well as the third finger, is on the 1st string, because only the note held down by the third finger will sound when the strings are played. Some chords such as A ♭ major and A ♭ minor for instance, show the first finger pressing down several strings. For this type of chord you should lay the first finger flat across all six strings and then place the other fingers where indicated. It will not matter that the first finger is on all six strings because other fingers are producing the notes needed. You will undoubtedly find this difficult at first, but with lots of practice you will master it, but it does take time, so persevere and be patient. Here is the list of Basic chords

A

MAJOR
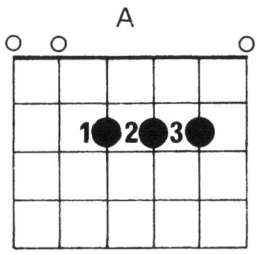

MINOR
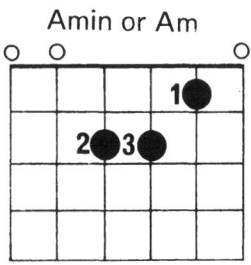

SEVENTH
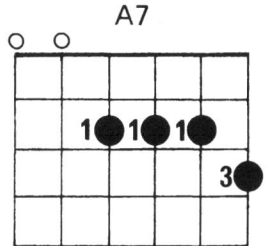

AUGMENTED
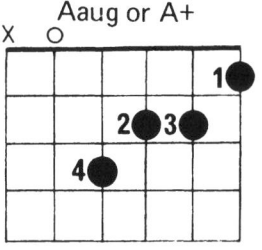

DIMINISHED
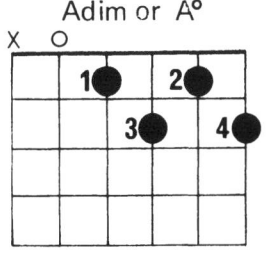

A♭

MAJOR

A♭

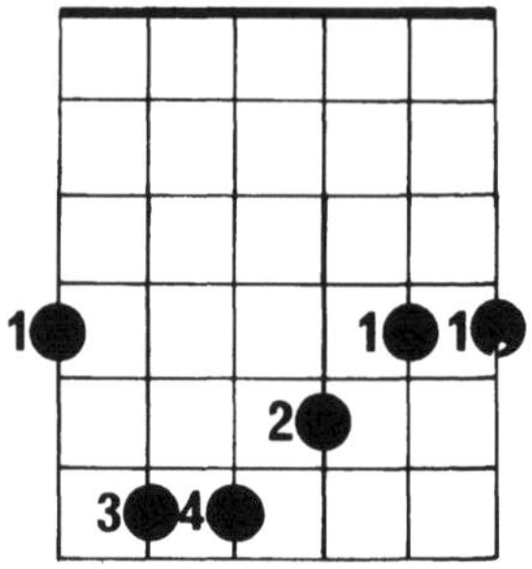

MINOR

A♭min or A♭m

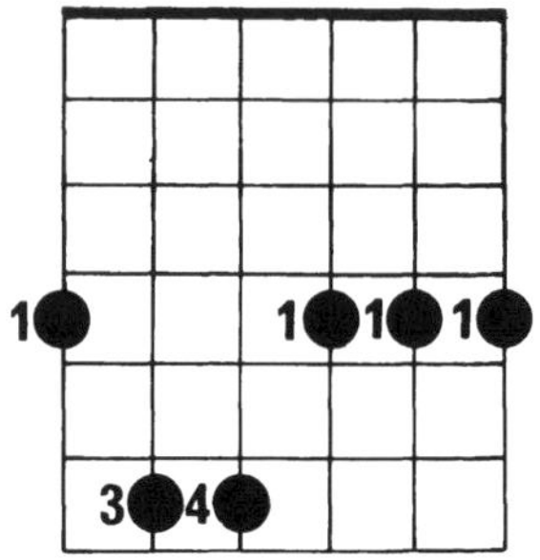

SEVENTH

A♭7

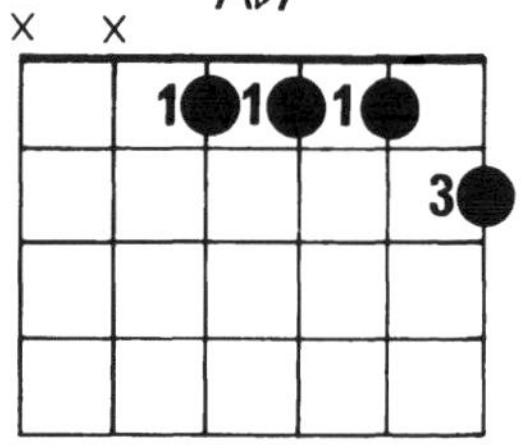

AUGMENTED

A aug or A♭+

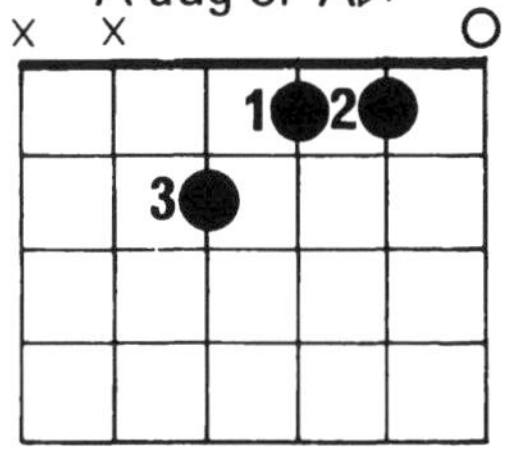

DIMINISHED

A♭dim or A♭°

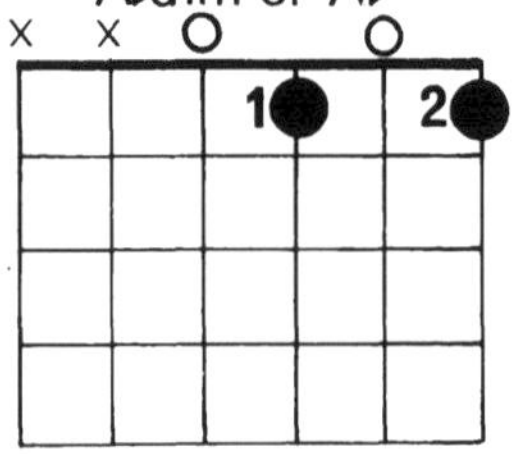

MAJOR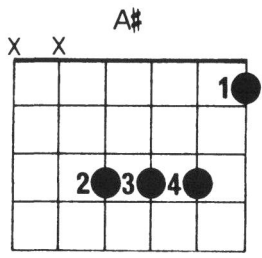

MINOR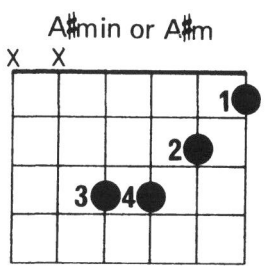

SEVENTH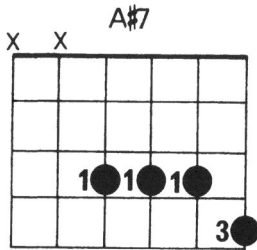

AUGMENTED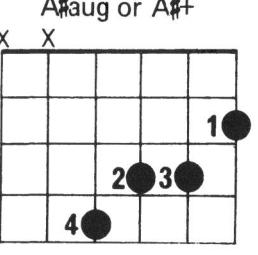

DIMINISHED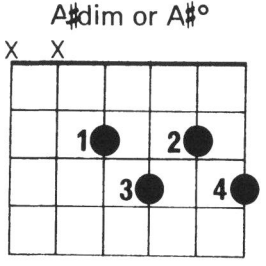

B

MAJOR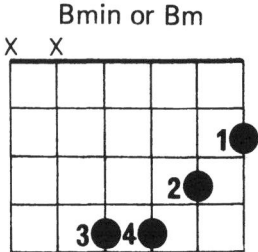

MINOR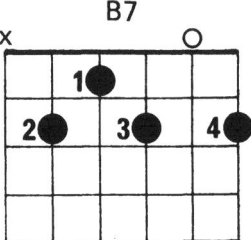

SEVENTH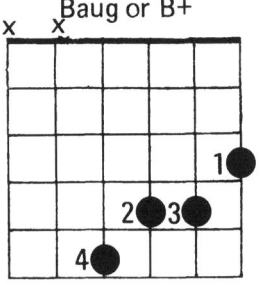

AUGMENTED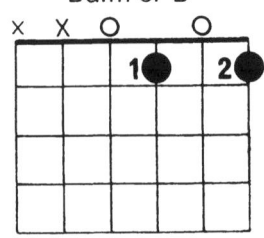

DIMINISHED

B♭

MAJOR

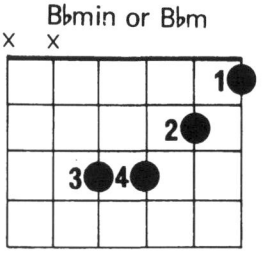

MINOR

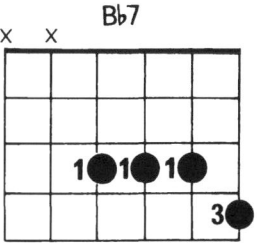

SEVENTH

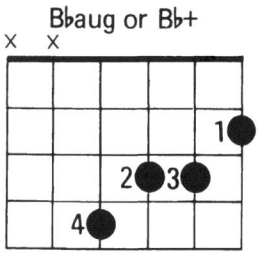

AUGMENTED

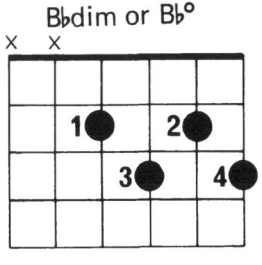

DIMINISHED

C

MAJOR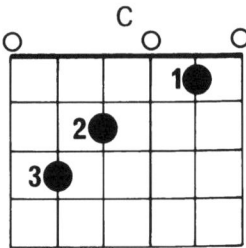

MINOR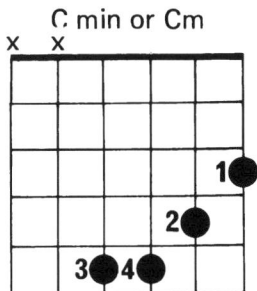

SEVENTH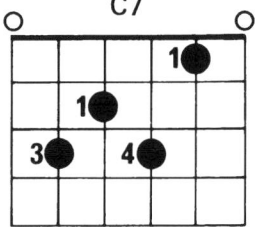

AUGMENTED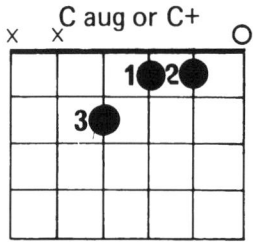

DIMINISHED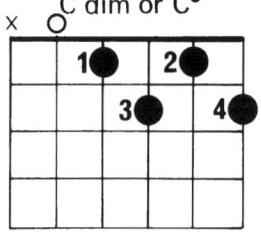

MAJOR
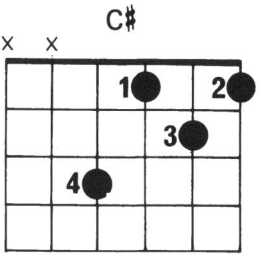

MINOR
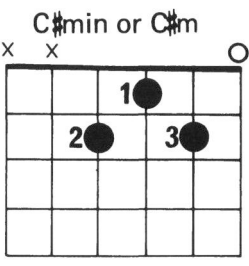

SEVENTH
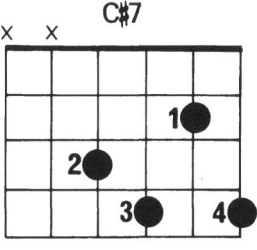

AUGMENTED
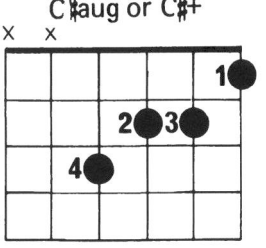

DIMINISHED
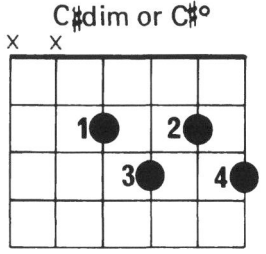

D

MAJOR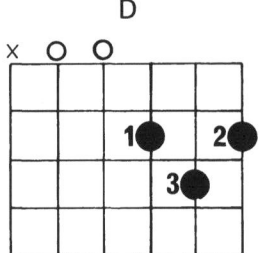

MINOR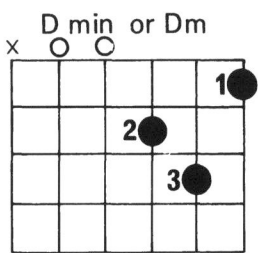

SEVENTH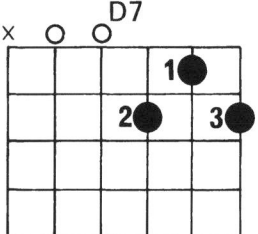

AUGMENTED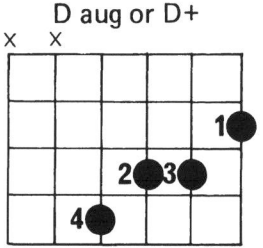

DIMINISHED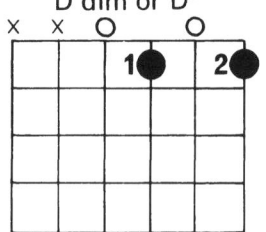

D♭

MAJOR

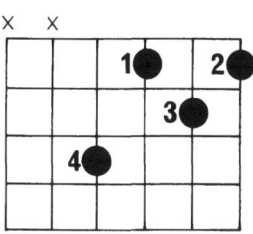

MINOR

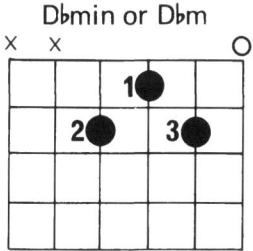

SEVENTH

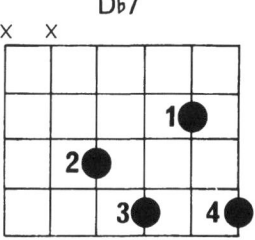

AUGMENTED

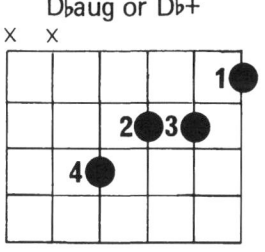

DIMINISHED

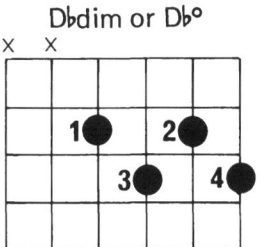

D#

MAJOR
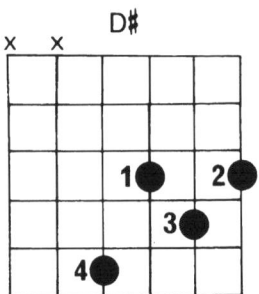

MINOR
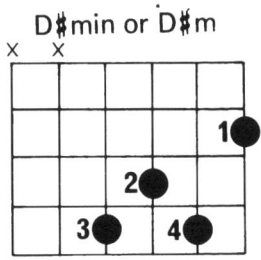

SEVENTH
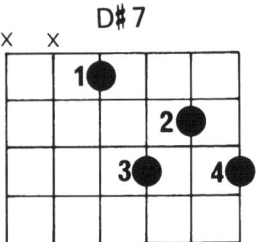

AUGMENTED
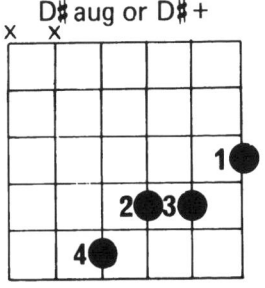

DIMINISHED
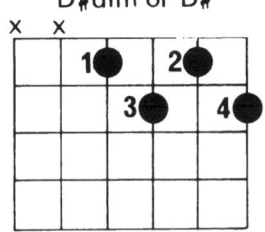

E

MAJOR

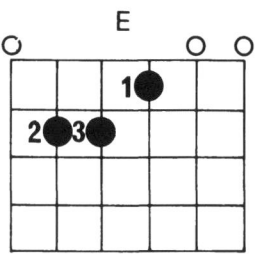

MINOR

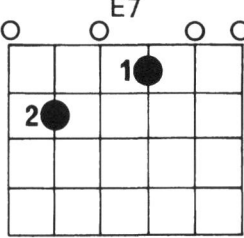

SEVENTH

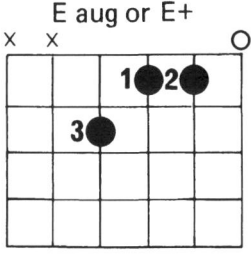

AUGMENTED

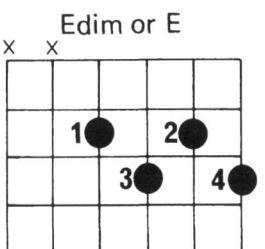

DIMINISHED

E♭

MAJOR

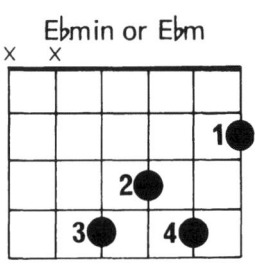

MINOR

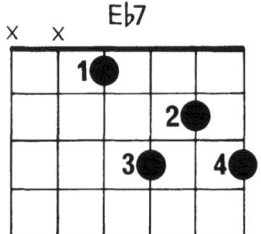

SEVENTH

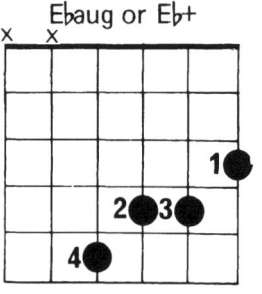

AUGMENTED

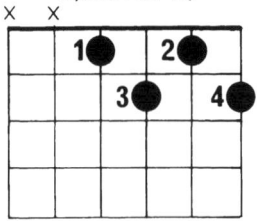

DIMINISHED

F

MAJOR

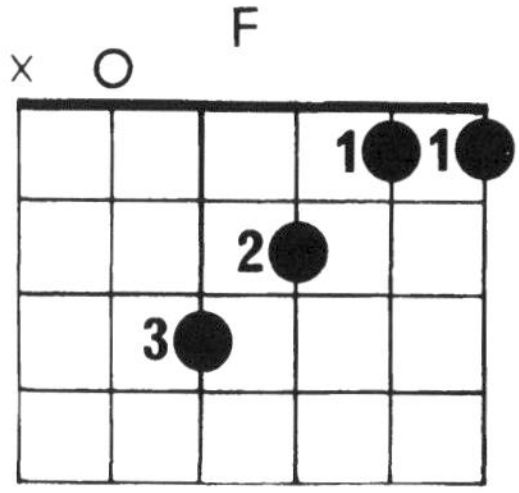

F

MINOR

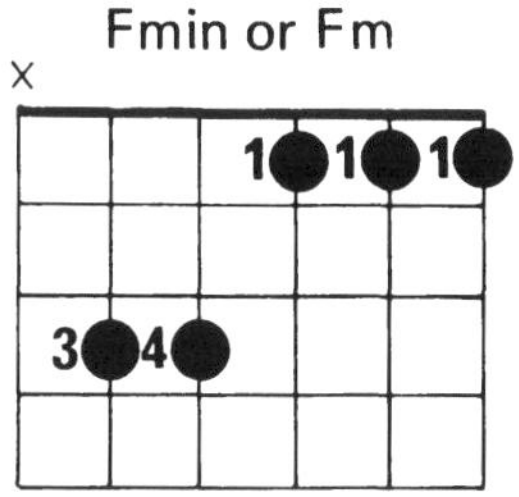

Fmin or Fm

SEVENTH

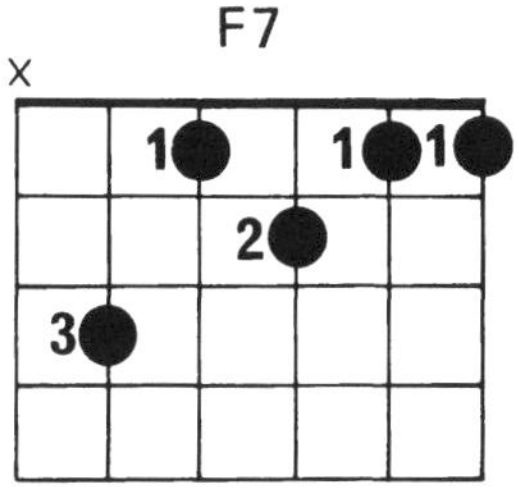

F7

AUGMENTED

F aug or F+

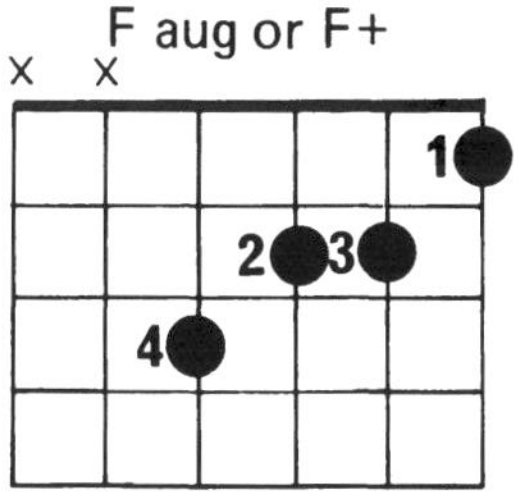

DIMINISHED

Fdim or F°

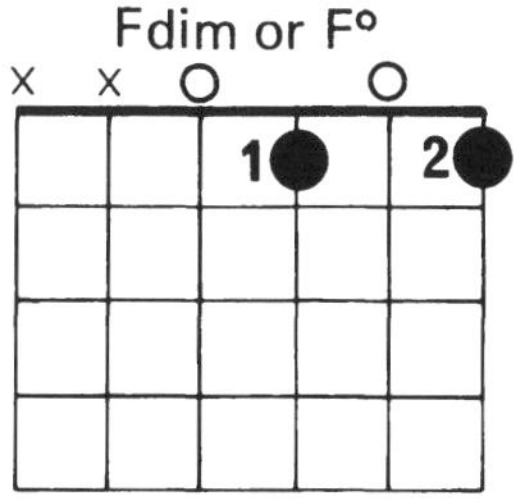

F#

MAJOR

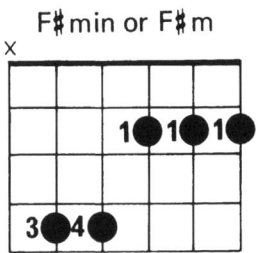

MINOR

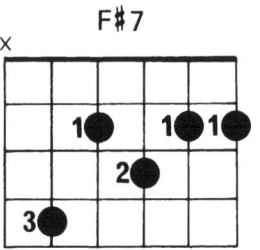

SEVENTH

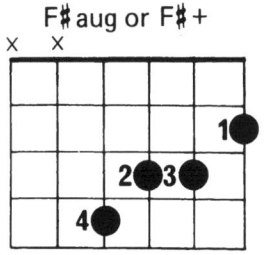

AUGMENTED

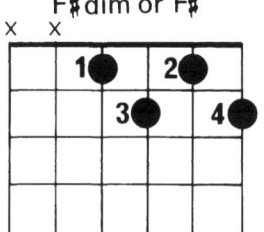

DIMINISHED

MAJOR

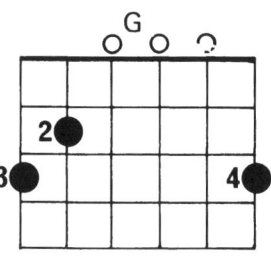

MINOR

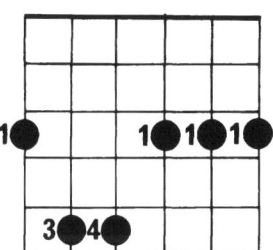

SEVENTH

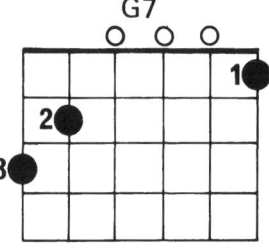

AUGMENTED

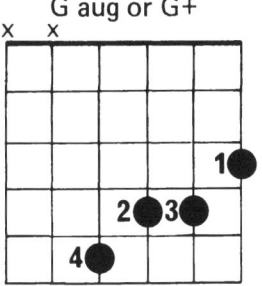

DIMINISHED

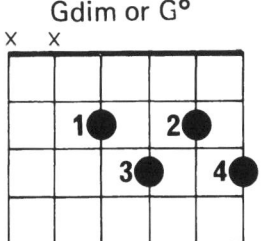

G♭

MAJOR — G♭

MINOR — G♭min or G♭m

SEVENTH — G♭7

AUGMENTED — G♭aug or G♭+

DIMINISHED — G♭dim or G♭

G#

MAJOR
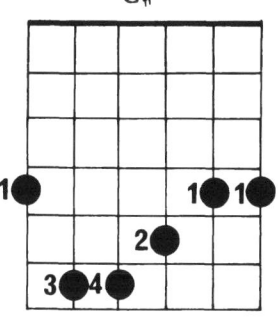

MINOR
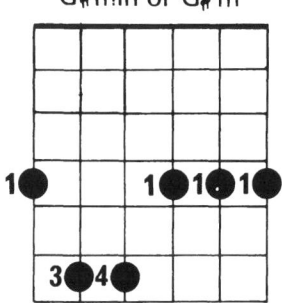

SEVENTH
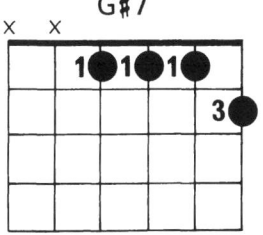

AUGMENTED
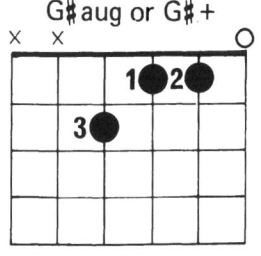

DIMINISHED
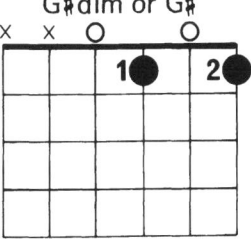

Part 3

Extended Chords

This section consists mainly of diagrams — of the extended chords alongside the basic alternatives on which they are built. Remember that basic chords can be played as alternatives to the extended ones **except for chords which include a flattened fifth.** (These are shown in boxed-in diagrams.) In all other cases it is quite acceptable for a beginner to substitute a basic chord for an extended one. The reader will notice that some of the Basic chord shapes shown in this section are different from those shown in Part 2. This is so that you might have a wider choice of basic chords to choose from when playing.

Apart from all the chords shown in Part 3 of this book, the student will sometimes come across even more complicated extended chords. Here are a few examples of such chords. I suggest that until such times as the student has an extensive knowledge of harmony etc., he should substitute the simple alternatives I have indicated for any chords not shown in this book. In the following list the letter A is used as an example but the same rule will of course apply to any note or letter.

For A9♭5 (A9⁻5) play A7♭5
    A9⁺(A9aug5) play A7⁺5
    A7♭9 (A7⁻9) play A7
    A11 play A7
    Am9 play Am7

EXTENDED CHORDS

Basic Chord Alternatives

A6
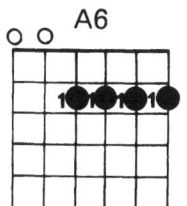

Amaj7
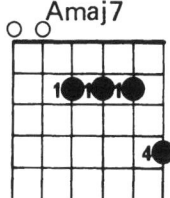

A
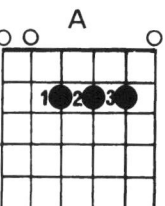

Am6
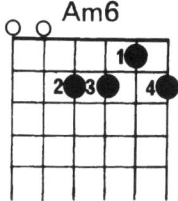

Am7
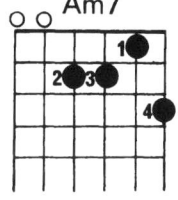

Am7♭5
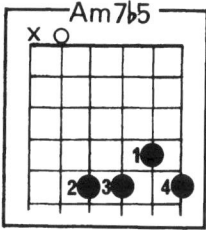

Amin
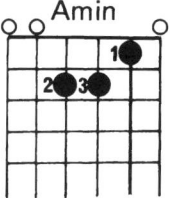

A9
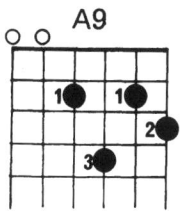

A13
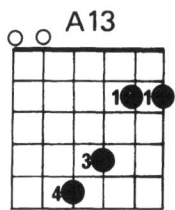

A7♭5
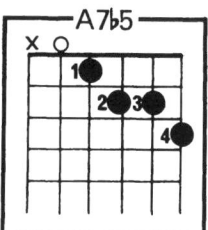

A7
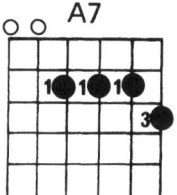

A7+
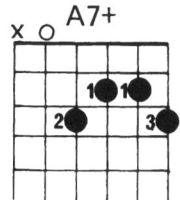

A+
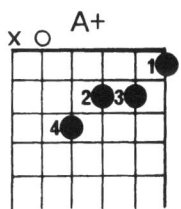

Adim
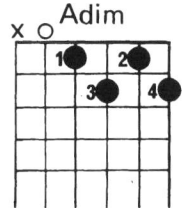

A♭

EXTENDED CHORDS

Basic Chord Alternatives

A♭6
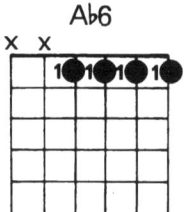

A♭maj7
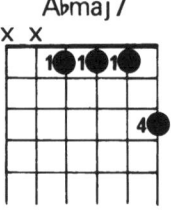

A♭maj9
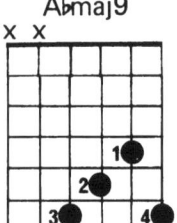

A♭
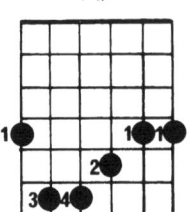

A♭m6
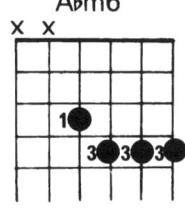

A♭m7
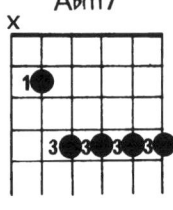

A♭m7♭5
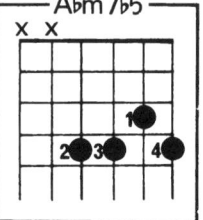

A♭min
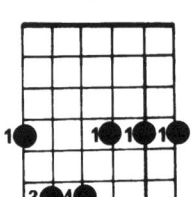

A♭9
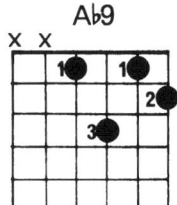

A♭13
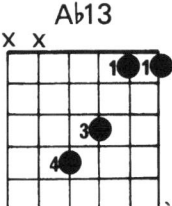

A♭7♭5
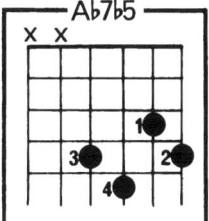

A♭7
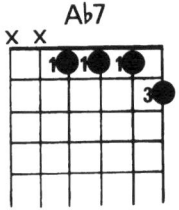

A♭7+
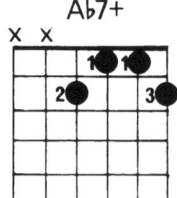

A♭+
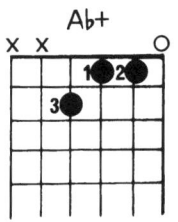

A♭dim
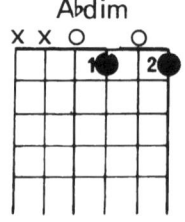

A#

EXTENDED CHORDS

A#6
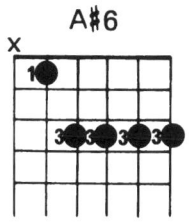

A#maj7
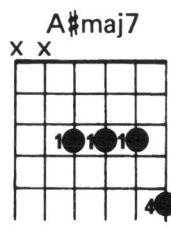

A#maj9
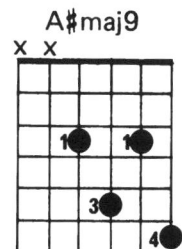

A#m6
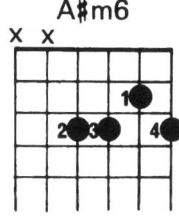

A#m7
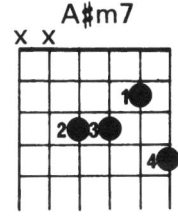

A#m7b5
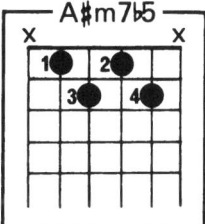

A#9
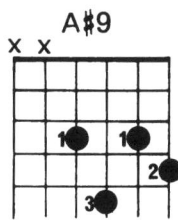

A#13
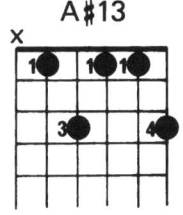

A#7b5
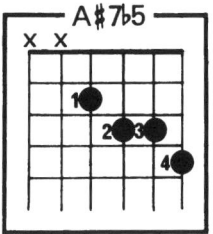

A7#+
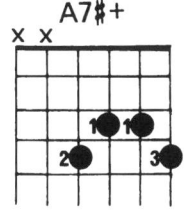

Basic Chord Alternatives

A#
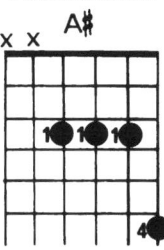

A#min
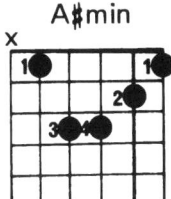

A#7
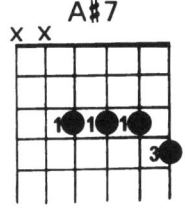

A#+
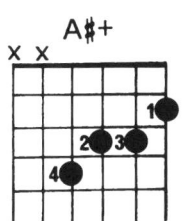

A#dim
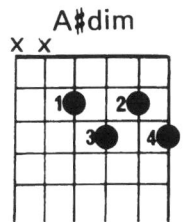

EXTENDED CHORDS

B6
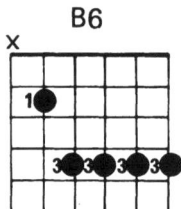

Bmaj7
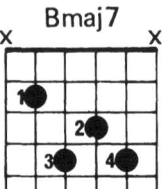

Bmaj9
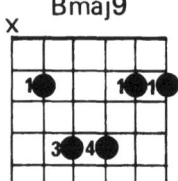

Bm6
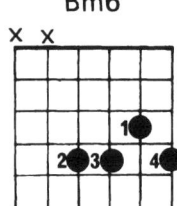

Bm7
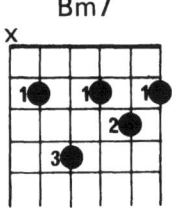

Bm7♭5
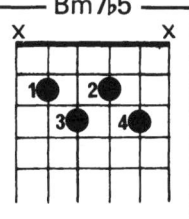

B9
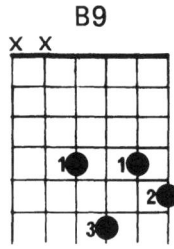

B13
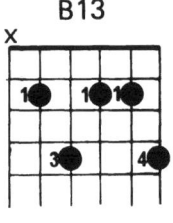

B7♭5
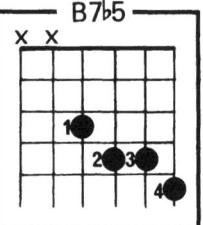

B7+
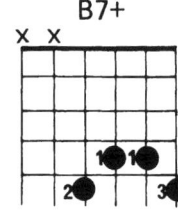

Basic Chord Alternatives

B
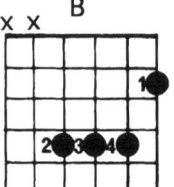

Bmin
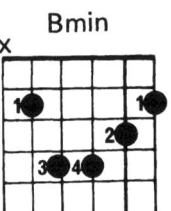

B7
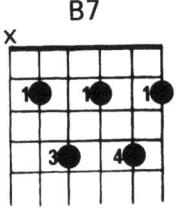

B+
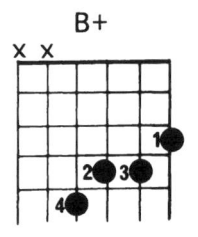

Bdim
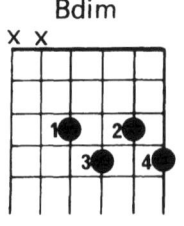

B♭

EXTENDED CHORDS

B♭6
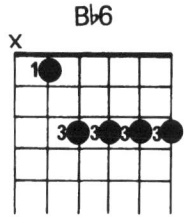

B♭maj7
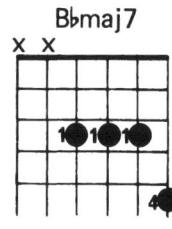

B♭maj9
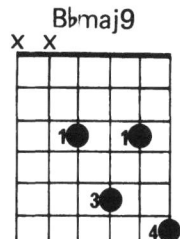

B♭m6
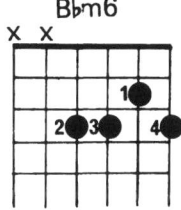

B♭m7
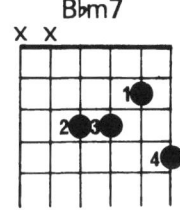

B♭m7♭5
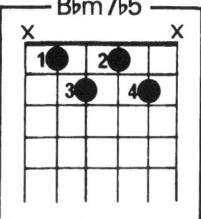

B♭9
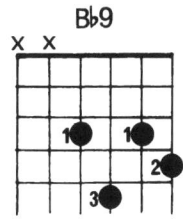

B♭13
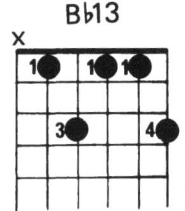

B♭7♭5
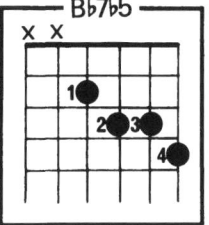

B♭7+
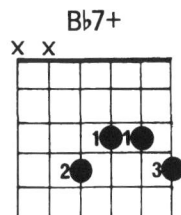

Basic Chord Alternatives

B♭
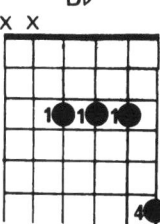

B♭min
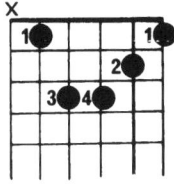

B♭7
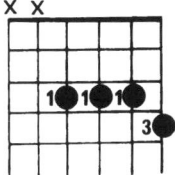

B♭+
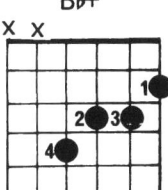

B♭dim
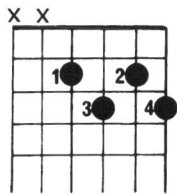

C

EXTENDED CHORDS

Basic Chord Alternatives

C6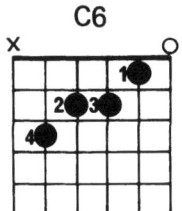

Cmaj7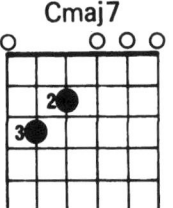

Cmaj9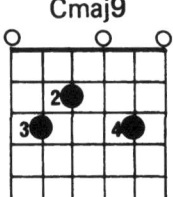

C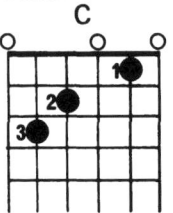

Cm6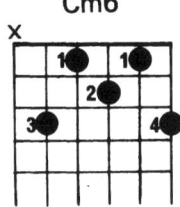

Cm7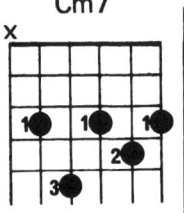

Cm7♭5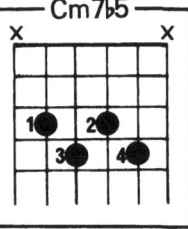

Cmin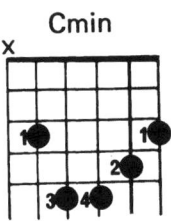

C9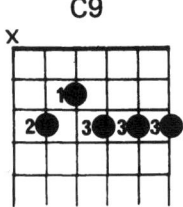

C13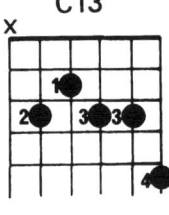

C7♭5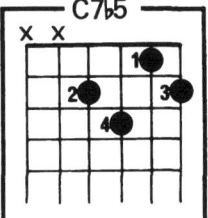

C7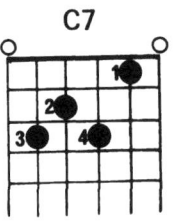

C7+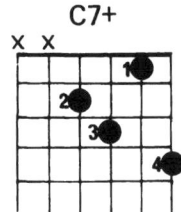

C+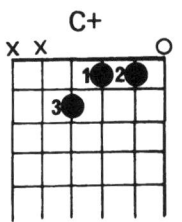

Cdim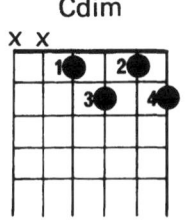

C#

EXTENDED CHORDS

C#6
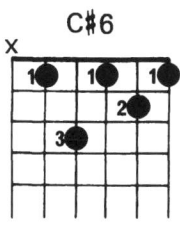

C#maj7
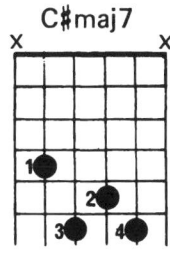

C#maj9
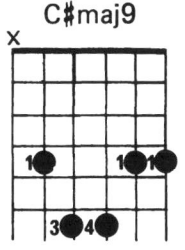

C#m6
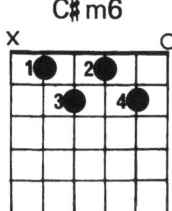

C#m7
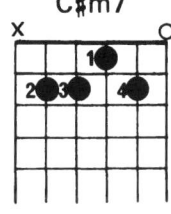

C#m7♭5
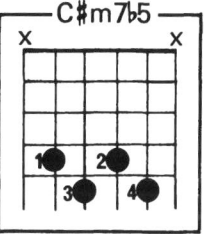

C#9
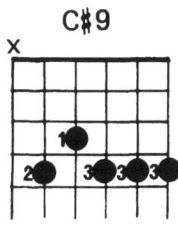

C#13
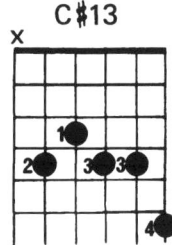

C#7♭5
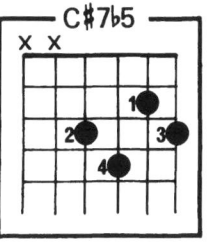

C#7+
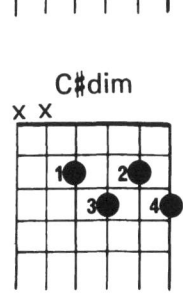

Basic Chord Alternatives

C#
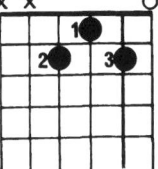

C#min

C#7

C#+

C#dim
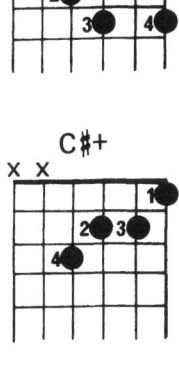

D

EXTENDED CHORDS

D6
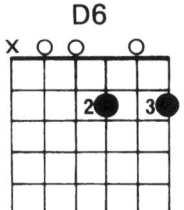

Dmaj7
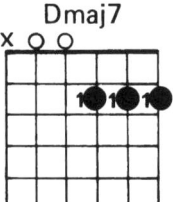

Dmaj9
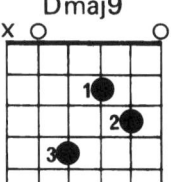

Dm6
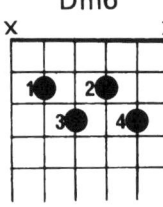

Dm7
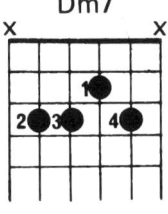

Dm7♭5
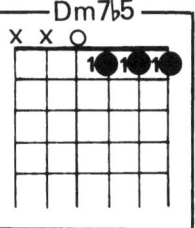

D9
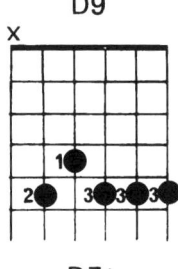

D13
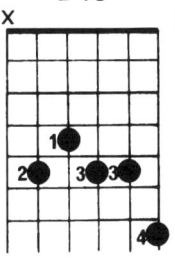

D7♭5
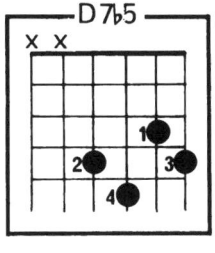

D7+
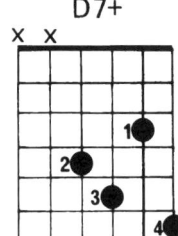

Basic Chord Alternatives

D
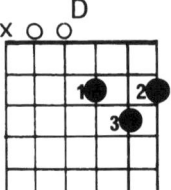

Dmin
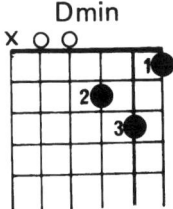

D7
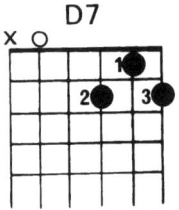

D+
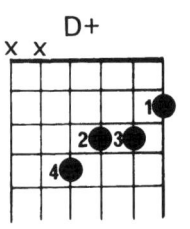

Ddim
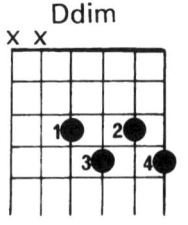

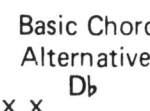

EXTENDED CHORDS

Basic Chord Alternatives

Db6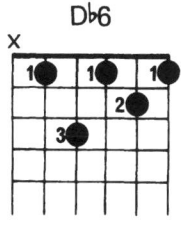
Dbmaj7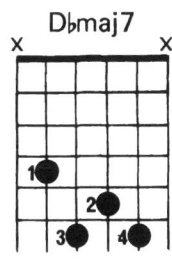
Dbmaj9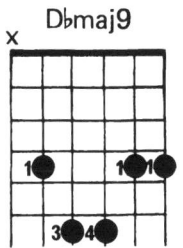
Db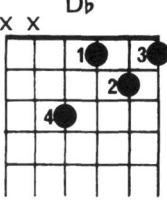

Dbm6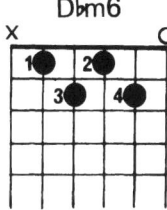
Dbm7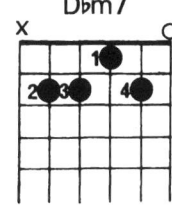
Dbm7b5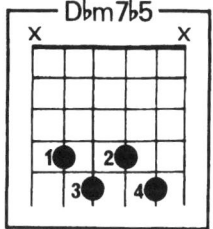
Dbmin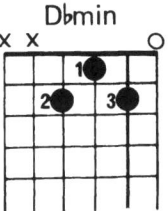

Db9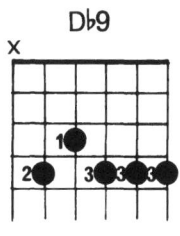
Db13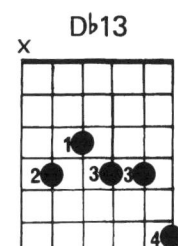
Db7b5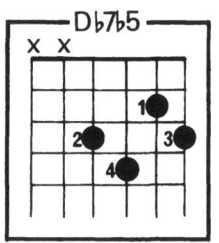
Db7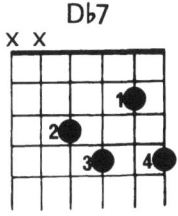

Db7+

Db+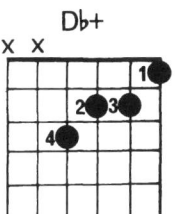

Dbdim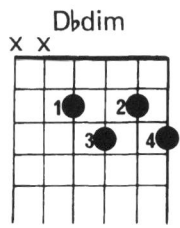

D#

EXTENDED CHORDS

Basic Chord Alternatives

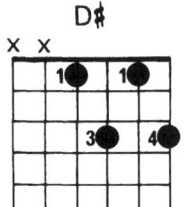
D#

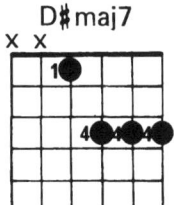
D#maj7

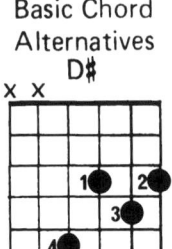
D#

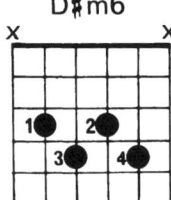
D#m6

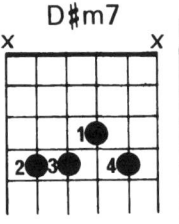
D#maj9

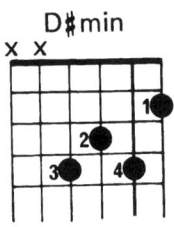
D#min

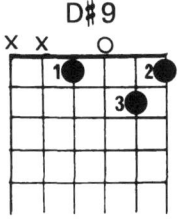
D#9

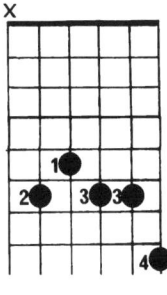
D#m7

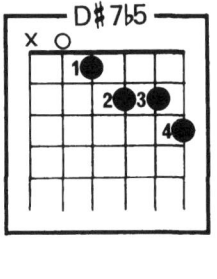
D#m7b5

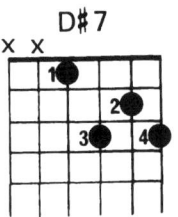
D#7

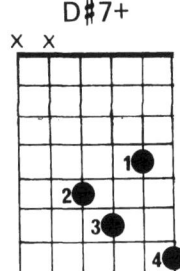
D#7+

D#13

D#7b5

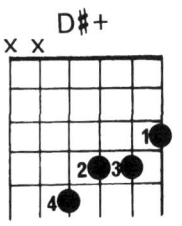
D#+

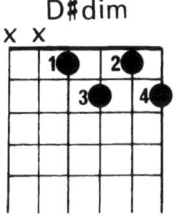
D#dim

EXTENDED CHORDS

E6
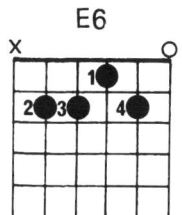

Emaj7
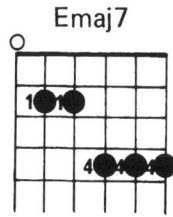

Emaj9
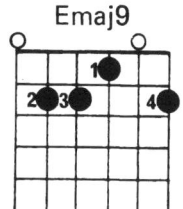

Em6
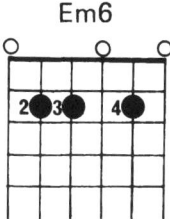

Em7
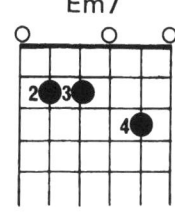

Em7♭5
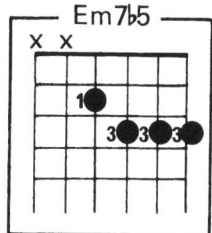

E9
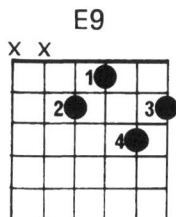

E13
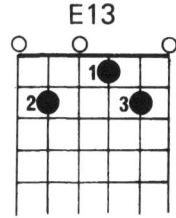

E7♭5
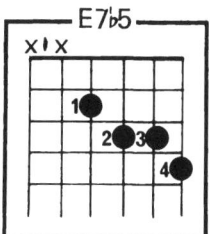

E7+
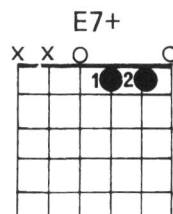

Basic Chord Alternatives

E

Emin
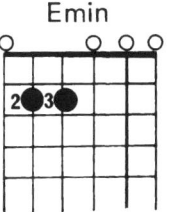

E7
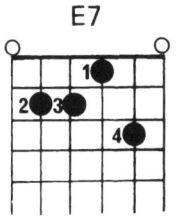

E+
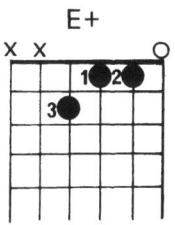

Edim
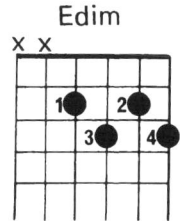

E♭

EXTENDED CHORDS

E♭
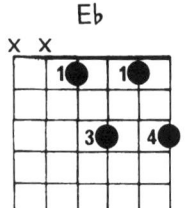

E♭maj7
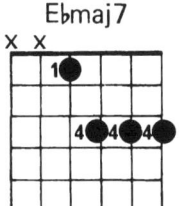

E♭maj9
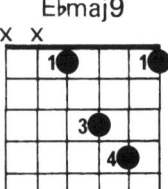

E♭m6
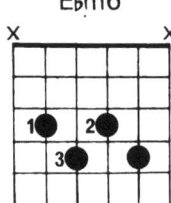

E♭m7
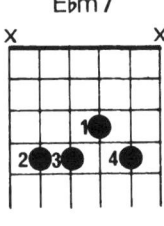

E♭m7♭5
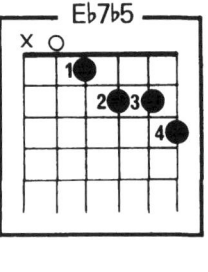

E♭9
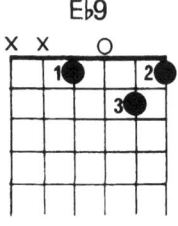

E♭13
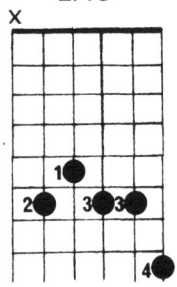

E♭7♭5

E♭7+
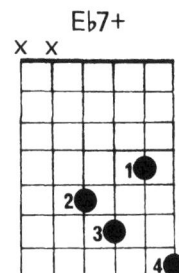

Basic Chord Alternatives

E♭

E♭min

E♭7
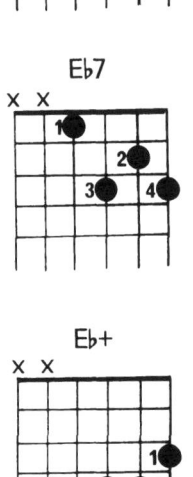

E♭+

E♭dim
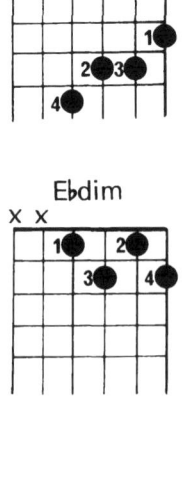

EXTENDED CHORDS

Basic Chord Alternatives

F6
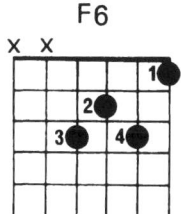

Fmaj7
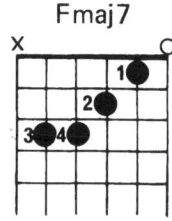

Fmaj9
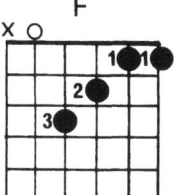

F

Fm6
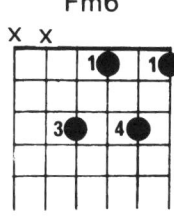

Fm7
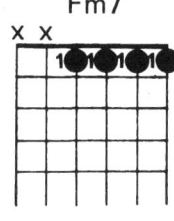

Fm7♭5
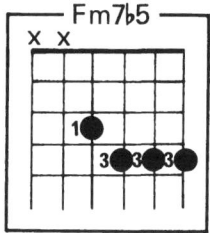

Fmin
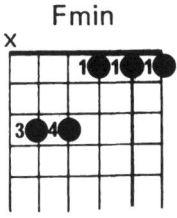

F9
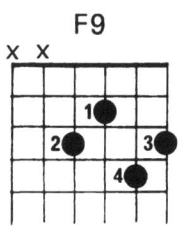

F13
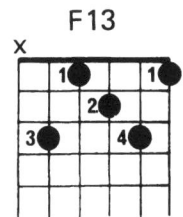

F7♭5
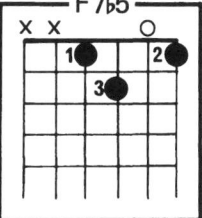

F7
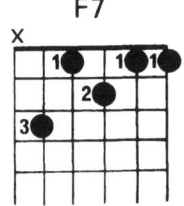

F7+
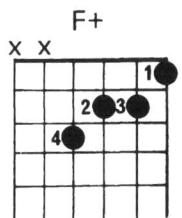

F+
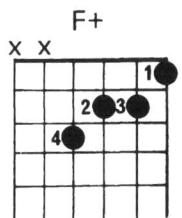

Fdim
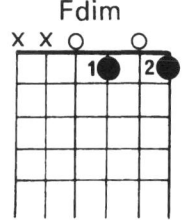

F#

EXTENDED CHORDS

Basic Chord Alternatives

F#6
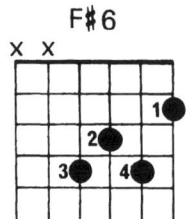

F#maj7
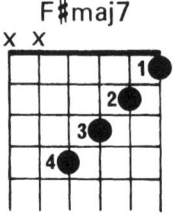

F#maj9
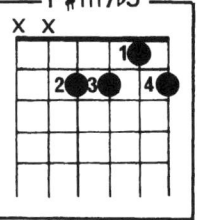

F#
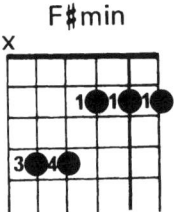

F#m6
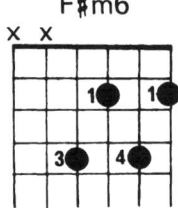

F#m7
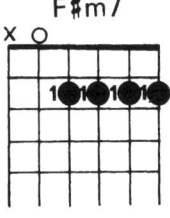

F#m7b5
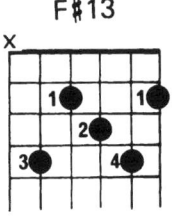

F#min
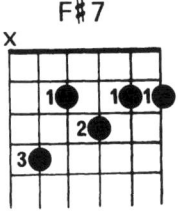

F#9
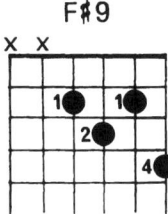

F#13
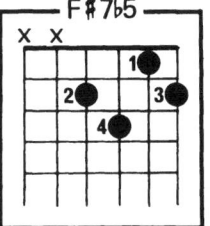

F#7b5
(shown with F#13)

F#7
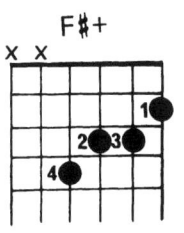

F#7+
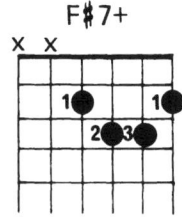

F#+
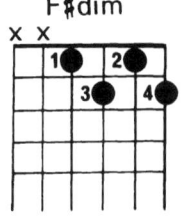

F#dim

EXTENDED CHORDS

Basic Chord Alternatives

G6
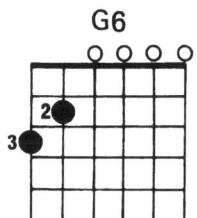

Gmaj7
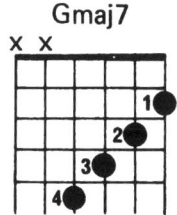

Gmaj9
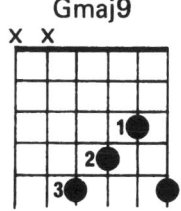

G

Gm6
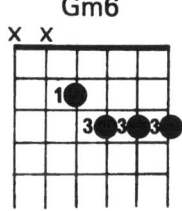

Gm7
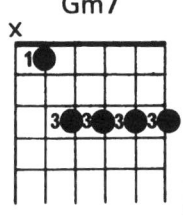

Gm7♭5
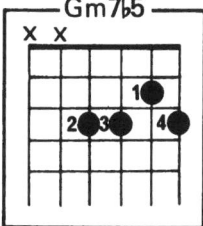

Gmin
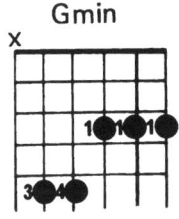

G9
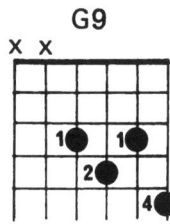

G13
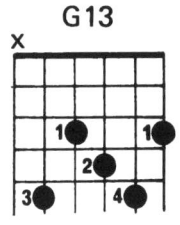

G7♭5
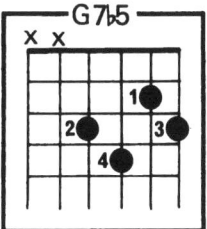

G7
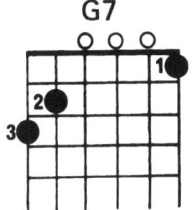

G7+
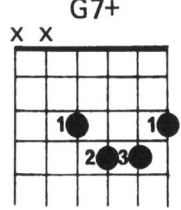

G+
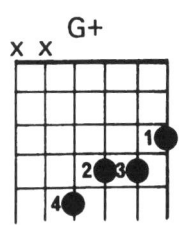

Gdim
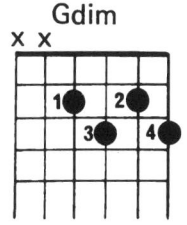

G♭

EXTENDED CHORDS

Basic Chord Alternatives

G♭6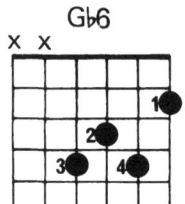
G♭maj7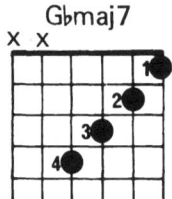
G♭maj9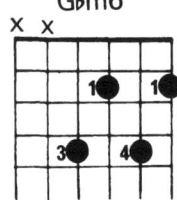

G♭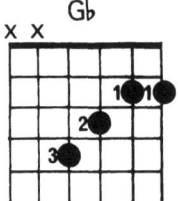

G♭m6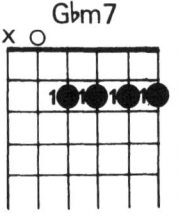
G♭m7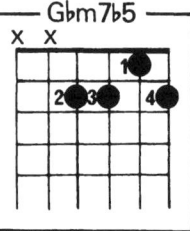
G♭m7♭5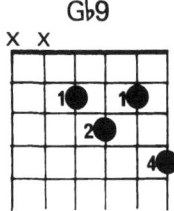

G♭min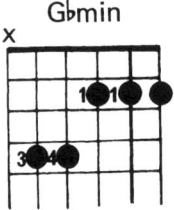

G♭9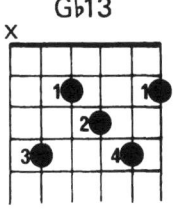
G♭13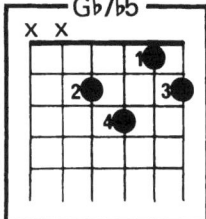
G♭7♭5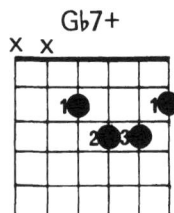

G♭7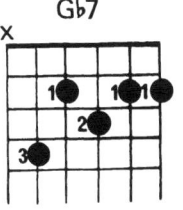

G♭7+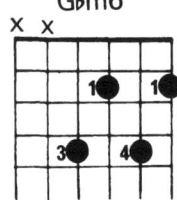

G♭+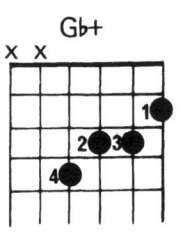

G♭dim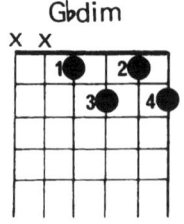

G#

EXTENDED CHORDS

Basic Chord Alternatives

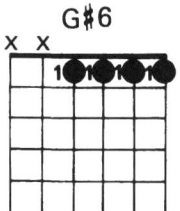
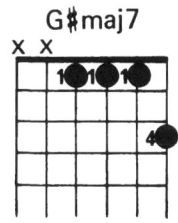
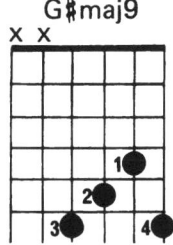
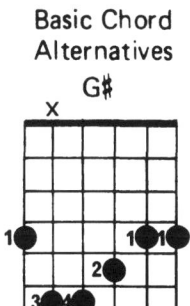

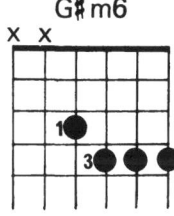
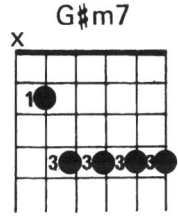
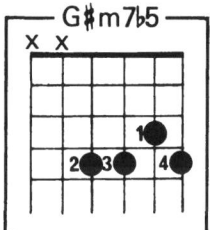
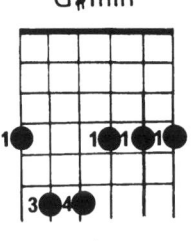

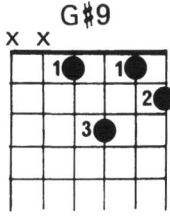
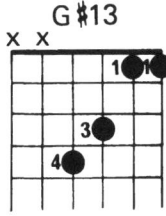
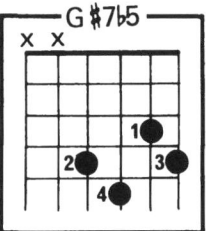
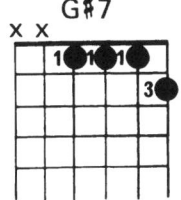

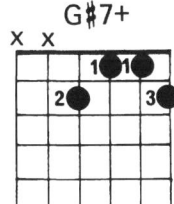
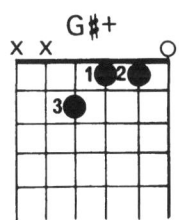

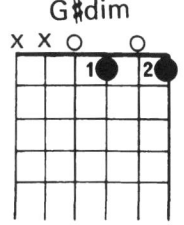

And in Conclusion . . .

I do hope that this book has helped, and will continue to help you with your guitar playing. As you will realise, the study and playing of the guitar is a lifetime job, for one never stops learning about music and playing it. Should you wish to go on with your studies I have written a book called **Play In A Day** which will start you off on the rudiments of music, and further chord playing, for there are many more variations of chord shapes that are played on the Guitar covering the whole range of the instrument. I am proud and honoured to say that many of today's pop stars have started their first steps through my **Play In A Day** book, and I hope sincerely that it will help you if you decide to continue to study this most exciting and lovely of instruments. Good luck, and I hope that you will give a lot of pleasure not only to yourself but to those who may hear you play because the guitar, in my opinion, is the greatest of all musical instruments. You will never stop learning something new about it and the more you know the more pleasure you will get. Listen to other players, play with other instrumentalists and singers, and your life will be enriched through doing so.